POLITICAL IDENTITY

W. J. M. MACKENZIE

Political Identity

MANCHESTER
UNIVERSITY PRESS

First published by Penguin Books Ltd 1978

Hard-cover edition published by arrangement
with Penguin Books Ltd 1978
MANCHESTER UNIVERSITY PRESS
Oxford Road, Manchester M13 9PL

British Library cataloguing in publication data
Mackenzie, William James Millar
  Political identity.
  1. Political sociology   2. Identity (Psychology)
  I. Title
  301.5'92   JA76
  ISBN 0-7190-0710-0

Printed and bound in Great Britain by
A. Wheaton & Co. Ltd., Exeter

CONTENTS

Words get tired quickly. Frequent use of the same phrase drains away its strength, and over-familiarity with a given term tends even to change its original meaning.

Stephen Hearst, 'Backlash situation language-wise.' (*Listener* 11 December 1975, p. 791).

Professor Herbert Marcuse

The author and publishers regret
the erroneous statement on page 62
of the death of Herbert Marcuse,
and offer their sincere apologies
for any embarrassment caused.

ACKNOWLEDGEMENTS

THE author wishes to express his thanks for permission to quote material from the following sources:

The Symbolic Uses of Politics, by Murray Edelman, by permission of the University of Illinois Press.

Politics and Symbolic Action, by Murray Edelman, by permission of Rand McNally Publishing Company.

The Sane Society and *Fear of Freedom*, by Erich Fromm, by permission of Routledge & Kegan Paul Ltd.

Stigma: Notes on the Management of Spoilt Identity, by Irving Goffman. Copyright © 1963. Reprinted by permission of Prentice-Hall Inc., Englewood Cliffs, New Jersey.

Lament for Great Music, by C. M. Grieve, by permission of Macmillan London & Basingstoke.

Blind Fireworks, by Louis MacNeice, by permission of Victor Gollancz Ltd.

Five Lectures, *Eros and Civilization* and *Counterrevolution and Revolt*, by Herbert Marcuse, by permission of Beacon Press.

Soviet Marxism: A Critical Analysis, by Herbert Marcuse, by permission of Routledge & Kegan Paul.

The Logic of Collective Action: Public Good and the Theory of Conflict, by Maurice Olson, by permission of Harvard University Press.

Aspects of Political Development, by L. W. Pye, by permission of Little, Brown & Company.

Collected Poems, by Dylan Thomas, reprinted by permission of J. M. Dent and Sons Ltd., and the Trustees for the Copyright of the late Dylan Thomas.

The Poems of Dylan Thomas, Copyright 1952 by Dylan Thomas. Reprinted by permission of New Directions Publishing Corporation, New York.

Part One

MURDER AND· DETECTION

THE history and structure of this book are complex, and the
reader deserves an explanation and apology.

The book began in 1974 as a seminar paper, a charade upon
some serious subject, to be played before academic audiences.
The charade opened with evidence that a word had been murd-
ered and took the form of a 'whodunnit'. The victim was the
word 'identity', an ancient word, which once had a certain
dignity. It was first harnessed to a dangerous topic in social science,
that of national character,[1] and was then driven out of its wits by
over-use. Stephen Hearst in the article quoted on p. 7 goes on to
say that 'linguistic fashion sometimes spreads certain in-words
among broadcasters like germs' – and among politicians too, as
has been exemplified recently by Professor David Watt and
Professor Sammy Finer in the *Listener*.[2]

The crime was easy to demonstrate, and it was not too difficult
to find the culprit, or at least a distinguished suspect. This
was Professor Lucian Pye of the Massachusetts Institute of
Technology, who played an important part in a very big
American research project dealing with *The Politics of the*

1. 'National Character is liable to be a pretty fraudulent industry, comparative National Character doubly so.' (Richard Cobb, reviewing a book by
Richard Faber, in the *Guardian*, 13 November 1975).

2. 'A Politician's Work', 13 June 1974; 'The Politics of Language', 13
March 1975.

Developing Areas.[3] The participators produced eight large volumes, from the late 1950s to the early 1970s, an imposing and prestigious example of American scholarship.

Thus one theme of my seminar paper was 'Where are the Gurus of yester-year?' Another was to exemplify the revival of a very ancient political metaphor in a new form. Pye explains that he borrowed the idea of the 'crisis of political identity' in new states from the work of the Danish-German-American psychologist, Erik Erikson, on the identity crisis of the individual adolescent (Erikson's work is perhaps most widely known in this country from John Osborne's play, with Albert Finney as Luther, first performed in 1960, which is drawn directly from one of Erikson's books).[4]

We all know the metaphor of the 'body politic': the identity crisis, then, is a metaphor not from body but from mind. A new state's mind is like an adolescent's mind. The weakness of the analogy, and its dangers, are obvious as soon as stated.

End of charade.

But by this time, I had myself been caught in the tangle of word and concept. The words 'political identity' had been eroded, but the problem remained, and could be stated in other words. Some of these are traditional; words such as loyalty, comradeship, honour, dignity, pride.[5] Clearly these cannot be kept within the bounds of the formal politics of the formal state system. It must include for instance not only nationality but class consciousness and other forms of social consciousness. In the end I formulated the verbal problem to myself as that of first person singular, first person plural; in what context do 'I' properly use the word 'we'?

I was (and still am) reasonably satisfied with this verbal

3. This is the title of the first volume in the series, edited by Gabriel A. Almond and James G. Coleman, Princeton University Press, 1960.

4. *Young Man Luther* (1958; Faber & Faber, 1959).

5. There is an interesting book on National Pride (*Vom Nationalstolze*) by a forgotten Swiss physician, J. G. Zimmermann, which was first published in German in 1758, translated into English in 1797. (It is shelved in the libraries among modern works on nationality.) This says most of what can be said about political identity even now.

formulation; but as I worked backward in the literature, I became increasingly convinced of the continuity and importance of the underlying conceptual problem. The words 'political identity' have been vulgarized, and are as useless 'scientifically' as their coevals, 'modernization', 'charisma', 'alienation', 'integration', and so on. But, writes Kenneth Tynan, 'We are constantly being reminded that language is a living organism, and that it needs regular blood transfusions of colloquialism and slang if it is to keep alive and alert.'[6]

Why sneer at the phrase 'political identity'? Why not use it 'properly'?

Clearly, I was in deep water; the rest of the book does not get out onto dry land, as I very well know. All I claim is that it sketches an argument and an agenda.

I was committed by the 'whodunnit' project to writing history backwards. The trail pointed first to native American work, in particular to the cultural anthropology of Boas, Kluckhohn, Benedict, Mead, and to the scrupulous social observation of Erving Goffman. What excited me more was that I began for the first time to read the work of the Central European exiles with some pleasure and understanding. These formidable and enterprising men and women (mainly, but not all, Jewish or part-Jewish) played an important technological part in, for instance, the development of nuclear weapons and nuclear engineering. They also imposed their specific cultural stamp on American social thought. The waters of the Rhine, the Elbe and the Danube poured into the Hudson and the Mississippi, and left them changed for ever.

The English, on the other hand, did not take kindly to rasping accents and stylistic Germanisms, and felt themselves closer to Paris than to Frankfurt. But their ignorance was extreme; and so is mine even now. But at least I have attempted to build a bridge back from America to Europe. The connections I have made are not the only ones. There were other German–American schools dissociated from the Frankfurt School; and French political

6. 'Percy, the Chutzpah of the North', *Listener*, 9 October 1975, from the Radio 3 series 'Words'.

thought cannot be comprehended in three names, Sartre, Camus, Fanon. But it is enough for my argument if I can show continuity in debate about a concept, which might as well be known by the label 'political identity' as by any other.

But 'Can these bones live?'

'The hand of the Lord was upon me . . . and set me down in the midst of the valley which was full of bones . . . and, behold, there were very many in the open valley; and, lo, they were very dry.'[7] An odd twist for a 'whodunnit', from crime to burial to resuscitation, and it was perhaps foolhardy to attempt it. But Part Three at least sketches an argument: 'There was a noise, and behold a shaking, and the bones came together, bone to his bone.' The argument, I know, lacks sinews and flesh and skin: yet I hope that it has movement. To be more explicit, I do not set out to tell the reader what 'political identity' is. But I think I know now where to look for it.

7. *Ezekiel*, xxxvii.

CHAPTER I
MURDER OF A WORD

> A man may take to drink because he feels himself to be
> a failure, and then fail all the more completely because
> he drinks. It is rather the same thing that is happening
> to the English language. It becomes ugly and in-
> accurate because our thoughts are foolish, but the
> slovenliness of our language makes it easier for us to
> have foolish thoughts.
>
> GEORGE ORWELL, 'Politics and the English
> Language' (1946), reprinted in *Inside the Whale
> and Other Essays* (Penguin, 1962), p. 143.

I SET out on this project with the idea that there existed a concept
called 'political identity'. If the word 'called' makes this sound
as if men name concepts as if they were naming dogs, make it 'a
concept of political identity', or simply 'a concept "political
identity"'.

The evidence for this was the proliferation of the term in
semi-popular discourse from about 1971.

Here are two good middle-of-the-road examples:

The Scots and Welsh have been aware of this for some time, hence
the growing movement towards self rule. This movement is nothing
more than a quest for identity – a quest similar to that sought and
attained in our lifetime by many former countries of the British
Empire.[1]

The enthusiasm for Ossian quickly shifted to Denmark and
Germany, where it became a very serious business indeed. Immediately,
the poems were identified as part of the teutonic mythology and
recruited into the struggle for national identity.[2]

I have comparable quotations for the E.E.C., China, Japan,

1. A letter to *The Times* from Ludovic Kennedy: printed 26 February
1974.
2. An article by Eric Rowe on Ossian, apropos of a Paris exhibition: *The
Times*, 28 February 1974. This quotation also has the word 'identified', in a
totally different sense.

East Germany, Canada, the West Indies, Israel, Palestine, Bulgaria, Algeria, Malaysia, the Tyrol, Singapore, blacks in Australia, Wales, Scotland, the Isle of Skye – and of course Northern Ireland. So far so good; the phrase is used as if referring with an agreed meaning to an objective phenomenon, and I set out at first to describe that phenomenon.

But circumstances grew suspicious. There was a heading in the *Glasgow Herald*, 26 February 1974.

SCOTS WANT THEIR OWN IDENTITY

Seems obvious, just before the General Election of 28 February ? But no; this is the Yachting column, and refers to a refusal by established yachting associations 'to accept an entry from a Scottish team of yachts for the One Ton Cup series of races from Torbay in July'.

The Music Critic of *The Times* (8 January 1974) reports that the New York Metropolitan Opera 'seems to be in the throes of an identity crisis' (this on the evidence of its 'new' production of *The Tales of Hoffmann*). The rugby football correspondent of the *London Evening News* (8 February 1974) blames the relative failure of London clubs in the national championships on the lack of a sense of identity in Greater London. By 1976 English rugby had deteriorated further: 'Everyone *tries* when they put on the white jersey with the red rose – of course they do – but you have to be able to identify with the character of the side, and we can't do that because the side has no character' (John Spencer, quoted in the *Guardian*, 9 April 1976).

The currency is in course of depreciation ? It was inflated further by the political rhetoric of an election. Here is Wedgwood Benn, who said:

after his adoption at Bristol, South-east, yesterday that he would fight the general election 'as a crusade for a fairer, more equal, and more democratic Britain in which we rediscover our own identity and try to re-establish our basic freedoms.

'These freedoms, these values and this identity, are all being directly challenged by those who now govern Britain' . . .[3]

3. *The Times*, 11 February 1974.

And who better fitted to cap this than John Enoch Powell?

He posed the question: Can the British people be prevented 'from taking back into their own hands the decision about their identity and their form of government which was truly theirs all along'?...[4]

It seemed then that the bubble must burst, yet Healey contrived a further puff: '... the final collapse and disintegration of the Conservative Opposition. They had neither policy, leadership nor even the vestigial trace of a political identity.'[5]

And finally, across the thin line dividing self-parody from diplomatic humbug:

22. The European identity will evolve in a dynamic way as the construction of a united Europe proceeds. In their external relations, the Nine propose progressively to undertake the definition of their identity in relation to other countries or groups of countries. They believe that in so doing they will strengthen their own cohesion and contribute to the framing of a genuinely European foreign policy. They are convinced that building up this policy will help them to tackle with confidence and realism further stages in the construction of a united Europe, thus making easier the proposed transformation of the whole complex of their relations into a European Union.

That is the concluding paragraph and peroration of a White Paper called *The European Identity*,[6] approved by the Foreign Ministers of the Nine and 'published on the occasion of the European Summit Meeting in Copenhagen on 14 December 1973'. Is that not the authentic flavour of Orwellian Newspeak?

One way to link this sequence of changing usage is through the traditional lore of rhetoric. An orator who wishes to carry an audience with him should attempt to establish a situation in which he can plausibly use the word 'we'; not my country, my interests, my traditions – not even your country, your interests, your traditions – but 'ours'. Benn does so, in this direct quota-

4. *Sunday Express*, 24 February 1974.
5. *The Times*, 'Parliamentary Report', 25 July 1974.
6. Cmnd. 5516 of 1974: there is a slightly different text in *Survival* of March/April 1974.

tion; we can bet that Powell did so, though the quotation was indirect. One reason why the European draft is on the face of it fraudulent is that there are no contexts (except the bureaucratic ones) in which this 'European identity' can be spoken of confidently in the first person plural.

I return later to this question of the appropriate use of the personal pronouns. At this stage, note only that the first person plural is the warmest of them and the most political; and that this inheritance of emotional colour has of late been annexed by the colourless word 'identity'. So far as I can trace, this usage of the word to refer to 'shared identity', the identity of a collectivity or social entity, has not yet reached the dictionaries. Is it a new label for an old concept? a new label for a new concept? or merely a with-it word, like 'alienation', or 'charisma', or 'modernity', used not to convey meaning but to give tone? A point nicely taken in a *Glasgow Herald* spoof:

I had lunch the other day with Roy Glenmorangie, livewire director of Growthpoint Scotland, the jobs promotion group. He was telling me about his search for a symbol for Growthpoint: 'We're looking for a sign which will express the Growthpoint philosophy and also embody our corporate identity. Basically, we are life-orientated. We try to operate at the job-environment interface' . . .[7]

The reader may like to test his or her skill on these two:
Headlines on the same page of the *Guardian*, 24 April 1976, for separate reports from Saigon:

VIETNAM NOW FINDING   DISSENT TO BE
ITS IDENTITY   WIPED OUT

The *Guardian*, 10 April 1976:

HAIN VOWS TO BRAKE IDENTITY BANDWAGON

7. 24 April 1976.

CHAPTER 2

LIFE-STORY OF THE VICTIM

> It is not only a matter of this meagreness of word and
> of thought. It is clear that even when words of repute
> and pedigree are being used, very little is being got out
> of them.
>
> ROBERT CONQUEST, *Words that Wouldn't Happen
> to a Dog*, from 'Words', Radio 3, reprinted in the
> *Listener*.

FIRST, can one learn more about the victim, its life and times,
friends and foes? I claim no special skill in lexicography, and
the story told here is derived mainly from the big dictionaries.
But it is an interesting one, at least for word-lovers.

The word 'identity' appears to mirror a Latin word *identitas*.
But there is no such word in classical Latin. If there were such a
word it would have come either from *idem* 'the same', or from
identidem, 'repeatedly'. So says the Oxford English Dictionary,
in a volume published in 1901, and it quotes usages in Latin
from the last period of the Roman Empire. But recourse to the
Thesaurus of ancient Latin[1] suggests a better story. In Greek
there is a convenient coincidence of the word for 'self' (*autos*)
and the word for 'same' (*autos* with a definite article); this is
'self' as emphatic (*autos epha* – 'the master himself said'), not
'*the* self' as a thing or soul. Apparently it was the master himself,
Aristotle, who coined a rather barbarous abstract substantive,
tautotes, rendered exactly into Latin by *identitas*, except that the
Latin is a word simply for 'sameness' without any aura of
'selfhood'. And the dictionaries point to a passage in Aristotle's
Ethics;[2] 'And brothers love one another from being sprung from

---

1. Vol. VII 1, p. 211, which cross-refers to kindred words, *essentialititas,
existentialitas, substantialitas*. To my surprise, I found nothing useful in
Ducange, the most accessible source for medieval Latin usage.

2. *Nicomachean Ethics*, 1161b 31; translated by D. P. Chase, p. 202 (No.
547 in Everyman's Library, Dent, 1911).

the same; that is, their sameness (*tautotes*) with the common stock creates a sameness with one another ... In fact they are the same in a sense, even in the separate distinct individuals.' In fact Aristotle says drily what Plato put poetically in the *Symposium*, in his myth of the divided beings who are in love united, who 'share an identity'.

To judge from the *Thesaurus*, the words *tautotes* and *identitas* were, in theological and scholastic Greek and Latin, equivalent, and were both associated with the interminable debate as to whether the Members of the Trinity were the *same* in substance or *alike* in substance. But when the word 'identity' emerges in English, the Oxford English Dictionary finds little evidence of this theological colour, and points specifically to two distinct though cognate uses.

One of these is mathematical or logical. An equation is distinct from an identity – not a = b but a $\equiv$ a; the latter tautologous, the former making a statement – but how does one 'prove' that statement except by reducing it to an identity or tautology? A parallel but distinct statement in the elementary textbooks of 'modern mathematics' is that a number system may include an 'identity' element.[3]

These usages have now diverged totally from the group of usages which concerns us here. But two early quotations in the Oxford English Dictionary provide links in the main chain:

The Identity of the same Man consists ... in nothing but a participation of the same continued Life, by constantly fleeting Particles of Matter, in succession vitally united to the same organized Body.

Consciousness always accompanies thinking ... in this alone consists personal Identity, i.e. the Sameness of a rational Being.[4]

Compare Hume's usage, in 1739:[5]

3. There is a useful technical definition of this, under Identity 7b, in the *Dictionary of the English Language*, Random House, New York, 1967.

4. Locke, *Human Understanding*, Vol. II, Ch. xxvii, para. 6 and para. 9. Quotations in *Littré* and *Le Robert* give examples of the same usage in Voltaire and Rousseau.

5. *Human Nature* (Book I, Part I, Sect. V). But compare this: 'There are some philosophers, who imagine we are every moment intimately conscious

Of all relations the most universal is that of identity, being common to every being whose existence has any duration.

These are the first quotations I know in which there is a move from identity as meaning sameness to identity as an essential element in the continuity of personality. Doubtless earlier cases can be found, but perhaps this is enough to make the point in general terms. It is one expression of the concern of old Heraclitus that *panta rhei*, 'All things flow', and yet there is such persistence that we can manipulate the 'things' intellectually. What is it that persists? Successive generations of philosophers have attempted to resolve the problem by re-stating it in idiom appropriate to the age, from Plato's eternal forms to modern games about language games; and there are many poetic statements, as in Wordsworth at his most Platonic:

> For backward, Duddon, as I cast my eyes,
> I see what was, and is, and will abide;
> Still glides the stream, and shall for ever glide;
> The Form remains, the Function never dies.[6]

There is also Goethe's poem called in German *Dauer in Wechsel*, persistence in spite of change, referred to by the late Ludwig von Bertalanffy in the peroration of his book *Problems of Life*, which modernizes the problem of life by posing it in terms of General Systems Theory:

> The river that seemed the simile of life to Heraclitus, ever changing in its waves and yet persisting in its flow, also gives final knowledge to Goethe–Faust. Incapable of looking at the sun of reality, he and the scientific mind rest content with a great metaphor, holding, however, inexhaustible powers of life and thought:

> Behind me, therefore, let the sun be glowing!
> The cataract, between the crags deep-riven,
> I thus behold with rapture ever-growing,
> Yet how superb, across the tumult braided,

---

of what we call our SELF; that we feel its existence and its continuance in existence; and are certain, beyond the evidence of a demonstration, both of its perfect identity and simplicity.' (David Hume: *A Treatise in Human Nature*, Book I, Part IV, Sect. IV).

6. 'The River Duddon', XXXIV, *After-Thought*.

The painted rainbow's changeful life is bending.
Consider, and 'tis easy understanding,
Life is not light, but the refracted colour.[7]

Up to this point, though the problem of personality is stated, the word 'identity' is still a word for 'sameness' and not for 'individual personality'. Yet it is difficult to see the point at which the metaphor dies, and the new sense is established as primary. Here are some cases from the Romantic Period, during which modern usage is inchoate. I happened on these quite accidentally and there may be many more. One is from Blake, quoted by Kathleen Raine:[8]

Distinguish therefore States [i.e. states of being] from
Individuals in these States.
States change, but Individual Identities
never change nor cease,
You cannot go to Eternal Death in that
which can never die

And Blake adds
"The imagination is not a State: it is the Human existence itself".[9]

There are two more in Byron. At the end of his journal in the Alps, he mourns that he could not lose 'his own wretched identity in the majesty and the power and the glory around – above – and beneath me'.[10]
And near the end of Don Juan (cxx):

How odd, a single hobgoblin's nonentity
Should cause more fear than a whole host's identity.[11]

7. *Problems of Life: An Evaluation of Modern Biological Thought* (Watts, 1952; German original, 1949), p. 204. Goethe poem from *Faust II*, B. Taylor's translation.
8. *William Blake* (Thames & Hudson, 1970), p. 207.
9. This is from *Milton* (Geoffrey Keynes's edition, Oxford University Press, 1966), p. 521. A glance at Erdman's Blake Concordance (Cornell University Press, 1967) shows how powerful the word 'identity' was in Blake's symbolic system.
10. *Encyclopedia Britannica*, 1901; Vol. 4, p. 480; author, Ernest Hartley Coleridge; quoting Byron's journal in the Alps, 18–29 September 1816, at the end.
11. L. A. Marchant (ed.), *So late into the Night: Byron's Letters and Journals* (John Murray, 1976). Vol. 5, p. 105.

From Byron's own reference to *Richard III*, this seems to mean 'substantial existence' rather than character or personality:[12] there is perhaps something stronger in the Oxford English Dictionary's quotation from Keats,

> His identity presses upon me.[13]

This was written as Keats watched the death of his brother, Tom, which foreshadowed his own death. But by 1820 the *Oxford English Dictionary* finds in Washington Irving a completely modern usage: 'He doubted his own identity and whether he was himself or another man' [*Sketch Book* I. 85]; a quotation which evokes the demoniac mythology of self and shadow, of the *Doppelgänger*, of *Tales of Hoffmann*, written in the years when Frankenstein and his monster were also born. The concept of a man's crisis of identity was familiar to the Romantic Age: but I cannot find a dictionary reference to 'identity crisis' before 1973, and even then the phrase is used of an individual not of a society (p. 25 below).

The verb 'identify' also foreshadows modern usage. One example is quoted by the *Oxford English Dictionary* from an obscure seventeenth-century theologian:

> our affections, which commix, coincide,
> and as it were identifi with that
> grandest and Divinest
> Mysterie of Love, sciz. God made
> Flesh[14]

And then there is a quotation from Burke in 1780:

> Let us identify, let us incorporate ourselves
> with the people.[15]

12. The *Oxford English Dictionary* remarks drily 'rare. ? Obs'.

13. M. B. Forman (ed.), *The Letters of John Keats*, 2nd ed., with revisions (Oxford University Press, 1935), p. 216.

14. *Oxford English Dictionary* under 'Identity', quoting E. Hooker, 1683; the O. E. D.'s orthography.

15. Burke: *Speech on Economical Reform* (World's Classics Edition, 1906, Vol. 2, p. 383).

As will be shown later, this usage ' to identify with' constitutes a logical bridge between an individual identity and a shared social identity, and it harks back to the classical tradition of rhetoric, how an orator should handle an audience. This is very well worked out by Kenneth Burke in *A Rhetoric of Motives*:[16] when should the orator slip from 'I' to 'we' and how is he to bring it off?

This is the essence of the present problem, as it appears in the rhetoric of Benn and Powell: but they are very far from Burke in their use of language, though not in the practice of rhetoric.

It would be plausible to say that Hegel, writing just at this time, bridged the gap from individual to collective identity: for instance, in this passage from the *Philosophy of Right*:

the *State* as freedom, freedom universal and objective even in the free self-subsistence of the particular will. This actual and organic mind (α) of a single nation (β) reveals and actualizes itself through the inter-relation of the particular national minds until (γ) in the process of world-history it reveals and actualizes itself as the universal world-mind whose right is supreme.[17]

The step is of great importance for the history of Western thought: the structure of man in society, continually cleft by alienation, the gap dialectically bridged by renewed identity. But I can find no evidence that the German word *Identität* was used by Hegel in that sense. It is true that later writers in German refer to Hegel as an 'identity-theorist',[18] but they mean something different though not unrelated (one should perhaps say that everything in Hegel is related); that for Hegel thought and reality are coextensive, though split by dialectical clefts which are successively closed and built upon by *Aufhebung*.[19]

16. Prentice Hall, New York, 1950, pp. 19ff, 55ff.

17. Knox's translation (Clarendon Press, 1942), p. 36. Compare the references to Hegel's Lectures given in Schacht (1971), pp. 43–4 (See p. 53, fn. 2).

18. E.g. Horkheimer and Lukacs, quoted by Martin Jay, *The Dialectical Imagination*, Heinemann, 1973, p. 47.

19. See the *Oxford English Dictionary*, under 'Identism': the word was thus used of Schelling in 1857.

I should like to be able to say next that the words 'identity', 'identify', 'identification' acquired a bureaucratic colour in the years around 1900. Unluckily one touch of the *Oxford English Dictionary* destroys the hypothesis: Blackstone wrote of establishing legal identity in 1769, Bewick in 1797 wrote of establishing the identity of a bird in relation to the standard classification of species. Nevertheless, the *Oxford English Dictionary* is full of examples of bureaucratic usage in the years from 1890 to 1920, and it would make sense to say that the bureaucratic state then reached maturity. There are two grim cases from that period; the need to register and identify motor cars; the need to register and identify each soldier in the mass armies of the First World War, so that his mutilated and rotting corpse could be identified by imperishable disc or tag. Undoubtedly 'the police state' had required much earlier (I have no evidence of date) that each citizen should be able to identify himself to the officials by his 'papers'. It is Kafkaesque that a man should become interchangeable with his file, *fiche*, or *dossier*: Kafka has gained power and relevance since his own time, because this experience has been intensified and has become universal. Hence Orwell's vision of the 'un-person', whose papers have been caused to vanish from the record. Hence the punning title of Nigel Dennis's extravagantly clever novel, *Cards of Identity* (1955), in which the bureaucratic theme is linked with a satire on the psychological theme, that an individual has identity (in the old Lockean sense) only in the eyes of others, and that they can manipulate it.

'Last scene of all
That ends this strange eventful history'

the lexicographers identify the usage 'identity crisis'. This is in *A Dictionary of New English, 1963–1972*, published in 1973,[20] and its two quotations are from 1970 and 1971. Here is its definition:

Identity crisis, a time of disturbance and anxiety when a person is in

20. By C. L. Bannhart, Sol Steinmetz, R. K. Bannhart (Longmans, 1973).

a self-conscious stage of personality development or adjustment, occurring especially during adolescence.

I am sure the phrase could be traced a little further back, in this sense, that of the identity crisis of a human personality. But there is no record of the now dominant usage, the identity crisis of a state, class, nation, or any other social group deemed to be an entity.

I do not wish to say that for the word this 'is second childishness and mere oblivion'. On the contrary I take it to be a sign of vitality, even of rejuvenation.

To recapitulate briefly. The word owes its origin to Aristotle, who uses it in a sense which is quite familiar though difficult, that of 'shared identity'. Thence it travels through late Latin and Medieval philosophy, being then concerned primarily with the central mystery of Christianity, three persons who are one person. I cannot vouch for the stages by which it slipped into English (perhaps also into French and German) as the label for a fresh problem of identity. *Cogito ergo sum* – 'I think: this implies that I exist.' But how at each moment of thought can I vouch for the assertion that the 'I' who thinks now is the 'I' who was thinking one nano-second ago? Without that assertion we have mere stream of consciousness, not identity (or sameness, or continuity) of person. The world of the personal pronouns crumbles about us.

There are thereafter at least four streams of meaning. One of these is logical and mathematical, and this cannot be brushed aside as being a mere technicality, since it represents a central issue in logic and in meta-mathematics. Do all logical truths, all number systems, depend for their force on a bare tautology, $a \equiv a$? Unfortunately only a few hundred people in the world are qualified even to debate this.

There is a second philosophical stream, for which it is convenient to use the peculiar word 'identism'. In its extreme form this kind of identity-theory obliterates the problems of personality and knowledge by eliminating the distinction of subject and object, 'the knower and the known'. It is generally said that

Eastern man can accept that; Western man cannot, except rarely and in moments of transcendence or of narcotic vision.[21] Undoubtedly this is Hegel's 'problematic'; probably it is best not to read him as an identity-theorist in the sense of 'identism', because he splits the manifold in two dialectically, by 'alienating' object from subject and by postulating what seems to be an infinite succession of splits and reconciliations of thought towards the Absolute, 'the intense inane'.[22] Identity, alienation, dialectic belong together in this context; nonsense perhaps, but not trivial. Hegel (as in the quotation on p. 24 above) perhaps went closer than any other philosopher of his time in attributing something that could be called identity to a human community. But I do not think he used the German word *Identität* in that context; nor in the English sense, which grew during the Romantic period, of the essential uniqueness, loneliness and torment of the isolated individual. It is apt that there should be relevant quotations from Blake, Byron and Keats; and one can be found in Dickens. But though the theme was launched in England (and one could claim it for Shakespeare and the Elizabethans) it grew weak there in the smug age and found better soil in the tradition of the European novel, from Stendhal (or even Sade?) to Sartre and Beckett.

Then, finally, there is the prosaic bureaucratic theme[23] of identity parades, documents, discs, tags, number-plates, thumb prints, the photographs in the file or in the passport. 'Who am I?' An electronic record in a network of inter-linked computers?

21. Timothy Leary, *The Politics of Ecstasy* (United Kingdom edition, Granada, 1970).
22. Shelley, *Prometheus Unbound*, III, iii, 204.
23. The old *Encyclopaedia of the Social Sciences* (1932) treats 'identification' only as an aspect of criminology.

CHAPTER 3

IN AT THE DEATH

Who killed Cock Robin?
I said the sparrow
with my bow and arrow,
I killed Cock Robin.

LITTLE or none of this was known to those who invented and popularized 'political identity'. Nevertheless, there is a story and a connection.

In the middle of the 1950s the American academic community became aware of the growing pace of decolonization. This was before the bitter American experience in Vietnam and at a time when 'the free world' was still dependent for its freedom on American aid. American policy favoured decolonization and was in a Wilsonian mood of sympathy for all new nations struggling to be free: America saw herself as 'the first new nation', in terms of the Declaration of Independence of 1776. At the same time, there was an over-riding American interest in the maintenance of strategic and political stability; and there were already well-established connections between American foundations and developing countries, particularly in technical fields such as health and agriculture.

These political concerns affected the Universities, partly by an independent awakening of interest there and partly by a flow of funds from various sources within 'the free enterprise system'. It would be an interesting exercise to disentangle the threads of intellectual history in that period, but for the present purpose it is necessary only to note that in the period after 1945 the first reaction had been towards the creation of 'Area Study Centres', in which different 'disciplines' were brought together for research and graduate teaching about various areas geographically defined: above all the U.S.S.R. and its 'camp', but also (for instance) Latin America, the Far East and Africa. As a result of a series of reports,[1] which apparently enjoyed strong Foreign Office support, the United Kingdom followed the American examples of Area Studies at a time when the Americans were beginning to discover inherent difficulties. These were, in particular, that 'the disciplines' came into each centre separately and that unification was difficult; that teaching courses lacked theoretical content and were apt to fall apart; that geographical areas were an unreal basis of analysis in a world increasingly interdependent. Hence a swing in the other direction, that of involving each discipline separately in the development of general theory in its own intellectual field; towards the sociology and social psychology of 'modernization', towards theories of 'economic growth', towards theories of 'political development'. This trend continues; but in recent years it has been met by a counter-trend, prompted by the violent events of the 1960s, towards a unified theory of the whole world-system. The last phase suffers from the weaknesses which were to be amended in Phase One and Phase Two; it lacks the precise local knowledge offered by Area Studies, it lacks disciplined theory, and it tends in consequence towards a rather shallow neo-Marxism. Nevertheless, the progress of American thought over thirty years can be seen as a single episode which has political and intellectual coherence. The bibliography is enormous and no one could master it all; there are certainly grave gaps in my knowledge even of the work done by political scientists, and I do not aim at a general survey even of that area.

The limited problem set is to trace the evolution of a concept (or verbal phrase), 'collective political identity'. The evolution was complete when in *Aspects of Political Development*, published in 1966, Lucian Pye set out schematically an account of the six crises of political development. The book is built up out of articles already published, but Chapter Three seems to have been written to give unity to the collection, and one may guess that it

1. A report on Russian Studies in 1946; then the Hayter Report on Oriental, Slavonic, East European and African Studies (University Grants Committee, 63–167, June 1961) and the Parry Report on Latin-American Studies (Department of Education and Science, 76–868, 1965).

was written about 1965. This is so far as I can get in tracing a single academic source for current popular or semi-popular usage. It can be shown that there were at least ten years of build-up to this precise and dogmatic statement. An odd thing is that this enunciation had no academic sequel. Of course it filtered down into the banality of routine teaching, and thence perhaps into the vocabulary of the intellectuals. But academically it withered on the vine; and there seem to have been two reasons for this. One of them was that academic research into personality and culture reached a dead end; another was that the political climate changed, funds and focus moved elsewhere.

A preliminary question is whether there is anything 'inappropriate' about the postulation of a collective identity, political or otherwise. I come back to this later in more detail and here I state only the *prima facie* objection. The phrase is a metaphor, moving from individual to collective. Chapter Two has illustrated the path of the word 'identity' towards the usage 'the identity of William Smith'. By analogy it is natural to write 'the identity of the British people' – or of Western Europe, or Nigeria, or Tahiti, or what have you. The analogy works superficially, but only at the level of cartoon personalities such as 'John Bull', 'Madeleine' and 'Uncle Sam', now happily obsolete. At a deeper level it is vitiated because it assumes what it purports to show. To quote the title of another of Pye's books: *Politics, Personality, and Nation-Building: Burma's Search for Identity*;[2] 'Burma' is in no position to search for an identity unless it already has one. Not so William Smith, who is from birth a person, though not perhaps a complete one. There is no proper analogy between the juristic conception and birth of a state and the physical (spiritual too, perhaps) conception and birth of a human being.

Here then is the key quotation:

Some members of the Committee on Comparative Politics of the Social Science Research Council have suggested that it may be useful to conceptualize the processes of political development as involving

2. 'A Study from the Center for International Studies, M.I.T.', Yale University Press, 1962.

essentially six crises that may be met in different sequences but all of
which must be successfully dealt with for a society to become a modern
nation-state.

The Identity Crisis. The first and most fundamental crisis is that of
achieving a common sense of identity. The people in a new state must
come to recognize their national territory as being their true homeland,
and they must feel as individuals that their own personal identities
are in part defined by their identification with their territorially
delimited country. In most of the new states traditional forms of
identity ranging from tribe to caste to ethnic and linguistic groups
compete with the sense of larger national identity.

The identity crisis also involves the resolution of the problem of
traditional heritage and modern practices, the dilemma of parochial
sentiments and cosmopolitan practices, which we have emphasized.
As long as people feel pulled between two worlds and without roots
in any society they cannot have the firm sense of identity necessary
for building a stable, modern national-state.   (p. 63)

The book then goes on to specify the five other 'crises'; those of
legitimacy, penetration, participation, integration (which later
disappeared – 'integration' became a bad word?) and distribution. Each of these 'with-it words' has its own history and its
own sponsors, but for the present purpose it is enough to note
that this is not a theory but a camel – a horse drafted by a committee. Each tag stands for a theory about what constitutes a
'mature' or 'modern' nation-state; each theory is interesting but
of limited range. Here they are simply juxtaposed, not unified.
It would be difficult, perhaps impossible, to produce a unified
theory of 'political development'; for one thing, the 'problematic' of such a project would be reflexive, it would be about the
role and potentiality of the social sciences in relation to world
events. Do they act upon events? or merely shadow them?

This crucial formulation corresponds quite well to popular
usage as now established. In particular, notice the slide from
'personal identity' to 'identification with' to 'common sense of
identity' to 'larger national identity'. This seems to be what we
want to say: the problem is to say it in a clear and unambiguous
way without loss of relevance and content. This Lucian Pye
has never done, to my knowledge; but he provides important

clues. He himself was born in 1921 in China of American parents. The reference works report that he is a Unitarian, so it is perhaps fair to guess that he was born into the American missionary tradition. He was educated at a good mid-Western college, Carleton, Minnesota, formerly Congregational, and then at Yale. Since 1960 he has been full professor at M.I.T., and he was closely associated (as the quotation indicates), since its inception in 1954, with the Committee on Comparative Politics of the (foundation-sponsored) Social Science Research Council of the U.S.A.[3] The Committee was active for some fifteen years, a long period in modern intellectual history; and, once again, it is a fair guess that Lucian Pye's persistence and energy played an important part in its productivity. Seven large composite volumes are on record; the seventh,[4] published in 1971, perhaps marks the end of a phase, not the fresh start which was required in the later 1960s.[5]

Pye's own published work falls rather strikingly into two parts. His first book is called *Guerrilla Communism in Malaya: its Social and Political Meaning*: it was published in 1956, and must reflect field work done in Malaya two or three years earlier, with the support of the British authorities, while the jungle war with Chinese 'terrorists' was still in progress. The book rests specifically on a series of open-ended interviews with members of the Communist guerrilla bands who had changed sides and were prepared to discuss their personal experience. In spite of the temptations to ground explanation on Marxist ideology or on some sort of quasi-Freudian analysis the book is strongly pragmatic in style. It attempts no general theory: it sees the renegades

3. Was the C.I.A. involved? Possibly: but the question is not relevant to a discussion of concepts.
4. L. Binder and others, *Crises and Sequences in Political Development* (Princeton University Press, 1971).
5. There is an excellent article by Donal Cruise O'Brien, called 'Modernization, Order and the Erosion of a Democratic Ideal: American Political Science, 1960–1970' (*Journal of Development Studies*, Vol. 8 [1971–2], p. 351), which sees a shift of emphasis in the late 1960s from 'modernization' to 'political order'. One could read this between the lines of the Binder volume (1971), but scarcely in its text.

essentially as pragmatic people, young Chinese trying to act expediently in extracting themselves from the dead-end of unskilled labour among a hostile Malay majority. They are seen as rational people to be understood in practical terms; there is a reference to the work of Erik Erikson, *Childhood and Society*, but in no great depth and in relation to the personal crisis of an individual, not to a crisis of Chinese culture in Malaya.

From the same period come three solid well-documented articles which extend the enquiry to the whole field of 'non-Western' countries; note the phrase, which by implication rejects generalization about political development, and builds on Area Studies rather than on Development Studies.[6] Then there is what seems from outside[7] to be an abrupt change of style and method in the book on Burma, published in 1962. For various reasons, I think this is a bad book – too much theory, rather incoherent theory, not enough patience in understanding Burmese individuals, a tendency to patronize the people of a very ancient civilization. This was the first conspicuous entry of 'identity theory' into political research, and (to my mind) a disastrous one. But it was mediated by the appearance of an article two years earlier on 'Personal Identity and Political Ideology',[8] a very perceptive account of the work of Erik Erikson on the crisis of adolescence, and the process by which a young person 'finds himself (or herself)' within a social context to which he or she contributes. Pye's work in general is solid,

6. See also in his chapter on South East-Asia in Gabriel Almond and J. A. Coleman (eds.), *The Politics of the Developing Areas* (Princeton University Press, 1960), the influential forerunner of the Committee's series of publications.

7. I should say that I have only once met Pye, briefly, in 1967, at a conference of American and British specialists financed by the Duke University Commonwealth Studies Center in collaboration with the Comparative Administration Group of the American Society for Public Administration and the Committee on Comparative Politics of the Social Science Research Council, at the magnificent Rockefeller Foundation centre at the Villa Serbelloni at Bellagio on Lake Como: a most pleasant occasion, but we were all prisoners of our own experiences and our own fixed positions.

8. In Dwaine Marvick (ed.), *Political Decision-Makers* (Free Press, New York, 1960).

careful, unimaginative: aware that the point of view of 'middle America' is special, yet blinkered by it. But in this essay he reacts sensitively to a sensitive and delicate analysis, almost as if it had come home to him personally.

So the next step in pursuit of identity leads to Erikson, who belongs to a different and more complex tradition, that of liberal Germany in the 1920s and 1930s. In the quest for theory Pye had got in deeper than he knew.

CHAPTER 4

A LINK MAN

> The shared beliefs and perceptions of a group and the
> individual's definition of himself are reflections of the
> same process: the formation of significant symbols
> that hold common meanings for all who are engaged
> by them. The formation of the self and the social
> interactions of the group are therefore the same pro-
> cess seen from different perspectives.
>
> MURRAY EDELMAN, *Politics as Symbolic Action:
> Mass Arousal & Quiescence* (Markham, Chicago,
> 1971), p. 53, referring to G. H. Mead.

IN his Foreword to the 1960 edition of *The Lonely Crowd*,[1] first
published in 1950, David Riesman writes of 'the current pre-
occupation with identity in this country (notable in the great
impact of Erik H. Erikson's work)'. Correspondingly, Erik
Erikson acknowledges Riesman's help in the Preface to his
Young Man Luther,[2] published in the U.S.A. in 1958. Each book
was in its generation a best-seller, and each has substantially
modified our common language.

Riesman was born in Philadelphia in 1909. His book was part
of a programme of research on national policy sponsored by the
Departments of Economics, Political Science, and Law at Yale,
and was primarily concerned with the relation between individual character and national politics in America: from it come
the three categories of man, tradition-directed, inner-directed
and other-directed, which became (at least for a time) vogue
words. Riesman's work interacted with that of Freudians and of
cultural anthropologists, but was highly individual and did not
found a 'school'.

Erikson likewise is an individualist, a man who backs his own
judgement. But he repeatedly and explicitly acknowledges
direct debts to two formidable schools, the Freudians and the

1. Yale University Press.   2. Faber & Faber, 1959.

cultural anthropologists. Each of these is complex and dispersed: but Erikson serves to focus what I believe to be the primary elements in the concept of identity.

Erik Homburger Erikson was born a Dane, in 1902, but his mother married again when he was young, and his stepfather was a Jewish (?) doctor of medicine called Homburger. Hence Erikson's second name, and his upbringing in Germany in the 1920s. His first training was as a painter: then he had a foot-loose period, as wanderer in Europe in the days of disoriented youth and deep economic depression. By accidents not recorded he joined the staff of an American progressive school in Vienna; became absorbed in his work with children; and proceeded to analysis and to training in psychoanalysis with Anna Freud at the Vienna Psychoanalytic Institute. He moved to America in 1933, and was then in the first instance absorbed into clinical practice, which involved some teaching. One of his earliest articles was on 'Hitler's Imagery and German Youth',[3] partly incorporated in his book *Childhood and Society*,[4] published in 1950, which was very widely read and has passed into common currency, through Lucian Pye and many others. As we have seen, his second best-seller, *Young Man Luther* (1958), became part of English literature through John Osborne's play, which follows Erikson's interpretation very closely.

These books are cautious, subtle, wise and elegant. Many of the exiles write formally correct English with overtones of German; the late Hannah Arendt for instance, who had important things to say, seems to have thought primarily in German, and it is often hard to follow her thought unless one can translate back into German words. But Erikson is one of the few exiles (Schrödinger and Michael Polanyi are others) whose style is English and carries no overtones of Central Europe. A consequence is that his work is not easy to summarize or to quote without context; when he leaves an ambiguity or an unresolved complexity it is wise to assume that this is not due to a language difficulty.

3. First published in *Psychiatry*, 1942.
4. 1st ed., U.S.A., 1950: 2nd ed., Hogarth Press, 1965.

The linguistic point is relevant, because he seems to have been the first to introduce the word 'identity' in the context we are now discussing. The concept to 'identify with' another person seems basic in Freudian doctrine, but it is said that Freud only once used the German word *Identität* 'in a more than incidental way'.[5] What enforced this new usage of an old and complex word?

As often, one finds that if one can state 'the problematic' one states the doctrine. Erikson accepts the Freudian techniques of introspection and interaction with the analyst. He accepts the doctrine of stages of psychic development, though with ingenious variations and formalizations of his own. (I fear that these influenced and perhaps confused Pye in his application to national crises). He accepts that the self can be understood only in terms of interaction with others. But there are important differences of sentiment and perspective. One of these is that without sentimentality he feels along with the feelings of adolescents: whereas many Freudians, including Anna Freud, his teacher, are primarily interested in young children, even in infants, and are apt to imply that everything is settled at or before the age of puberty. A second difference is that Erikson (to quote Riesman's words) is concerned 'with the liberation of men from the realm of charactero-logical necessity'.[6] He quotes Marx and Engels very little: but he is in effect transferring to the individual the famous statement about man in general:[7] that 'men make their own history, but they do not make it just as they please; they do not make it under circumstances chosen by themselves, but under circumstances directly found, given and transmitted from the past'. He fully accepts the insights of Freud and of many others about the ways in which people and events influence

5. See Erikson in the Stein, Vidich & White volume, p. 37 (p. 38 below, fn. 9), and in *Childhood and Society* (Penguin ed.), p. 273. This one example is in a rather notable passage, 1926, in which Freud discussed what he owed to his Jewish ancestry. For Freud on 'identification with' see 'Group Psychology and the Analysis of the Ego' (1921: *Works*, Vol. 18) and the *New Introductory Lectures* (1933).

6. P. xlvi of the 1961 edition.

7. At the beginning of *The Eighteenth Brumaire of Louis Bonaparte*.

personality. But he does not accept that they *bind* personality. He has been grouped with Gorer and La Barre as a 'childhood determinist',[8] but this is not confirmed by what I have read. A man makes himself, though often in circumstances of spiritual torment, constrained by the fetters of his birth and upbringing. Thirdly, it goes with this that Erikson has some special fondness for great men, and that heretically (though with much apology and precaution) he is prepared to introduce psychoanalysis into history and to 'explain' events in terms of people (Luther, Freud, Bernard Shaw), and to 'explain' people in terms of the struggle by which they 'find themselves'.

Fourthly, he is very reluctant to find pathology, either in adolescents or in historical situations. All young people, he might have said, are somewhat mad; to confirm that, one could pile up friendly testimony from poets, hostile testimony from the elders in every age. But they grow through it, and become fully fledged: this is a normal period of growth, dangerous but not pathological. Some are broken, and perhaps this has an association with schizophrenia. But Erikson was not medically trained and is reluctant to explore psychoses and their physical correlates. Some pass through 'normally' and become 'mature' and perhaps rather boring. Some pass through traumatically and become great men, great natural forces for good or evil: Hitler is one of his 'cases' also.

Hence the vocabulary of 'crises', which Pye abused in his attempt to generalize about political development. Adolescence ('that no-man's land between childhood and adulthood more or less derisively called adolescence')[9] is a crisis, and may be a very painful crisis. But it should be seen in perspective as one of a series of psychosocial[10] crises in human growth ('climacterics', in medieval terms); the disasters of growth can be understood only in terms of variation from normality – and human normality at

8. Victor Barnouw, *Culture and Personality* (Dorsey Press, Homewood, Illinois, 1963), p. 134.

9. Erikson in M. R. Stein, A. J. Vidich and D. M. White, eds., *Identity and Anxiety: Survival of the Person in Mass Society* (Free Press, New York; Collier-Macmillan, London, 1960) p. 84.

10. For this word, see Erikson in Stein, Vidich & White, p. 76.

times of crisis is troubling, torturing, even self-destructive. This is the price of manhood, of maturity, perhaps of greatness. To quote Pye's formulation, 'All people are to some extent creative, for all people must shape their worlds in finding their identities.'[11]

So far as I can see Erikson does not reject the Freudian myths of Oedipus and the rest, nor the Freudian model of id, ego and super-ego, nor the implied physiology of oral and anal stages and infant erotism. But in accordance with his voluntaristic leaning he sees the process of psychological growth as a sequence of chosen 'identifications', out of which a man in the end shapes 'an identity'.[12]

Undoubtedly in his later work, for instance in his article on Psychosocial Identity in the new *Encyclopaedia of the Social Sciences* (1968) he slides towards specification of the identity of a collectivity: 'a new identity of womanhood', 'a German identity', 'the passive Indian identity' which Gandhi displaced, even 'an all-inclusive human identity'. But the identity is still (so far as I can check) the identity which an individual can find through a collectivity; not the metaphor of Pye, that a collectivity can like a person have an identity and crises of identity.

11. In Marvick (1961), p. 307.
12. A final footnote: In his article on 'Psychosocial Identity' in the *Encyclopaedia of the Social Sciences* (Macmillan Co. & Free Press, 1968, Vol. 7, p. 62) Erikson remarks in passing on the 'faddish contemporary definition of identity as the question "Who am I"' Clearly this is not a definition at all: but it seems defensible as a preliminary Socratic question?

CHAPTER 5

PERSONALITY AND CULTURE

There is no proper antagonism between the role of
society and that of the individual.

RUTH BENEDICT, *Patterns of Culture* (Routledge
& Kegan Paul, 1935), p. 181.

THE vogue for 'personal identity' which Riesman describes owes
much to Erikson's charm of language, to his wide span of interests, and to his subtlety and flexibility of thought.

But it also had behind it the power of the Freudian movement,
though apparently Erikson himself was not accepted as Freudian
by any of the post-Freudian groups.[1] Any generalization is risky:
but perhaps the essence of his deviation is that Freud claimed
universality for his doctrines (even though he modified them progressively himself) whereas Erikson went some distance towards
'cultural relativism'; that is to say, towards the doctrine that the
structure of mind and personality reflects culture and is malleable
without limit. But it will be clear from the previous chapter that
he did not go the whole way: to do so would have been to re-
nounce Freud's enterprise altogether, to invite philosophical
criticism from diverse quarters (Marxist as well as Christian),
and (perhaps) to go against the empirical evidence.

There has been a tendency to contrast cultural anthropology
as an outgrowth of the American situation with structural (or
functional) anthropology as British, Durkheimian and colonial.
It is indeed true that the natural starting place for the American
study of mankind was close at home, in the extraordinary laboratory of cultures bequeathed by human advance through
America from the north through varying ecological belts; from
ice and tundra, by sea, river, mountain and prairie, to the high-
lands of Mexico and the jungles of Central America, where bar-

---

1. For instance, he does not even appear in the index of J. A. C. Brown,
Freud and the Post-Freudians (Penguin, 1961).

barian cultures reached the verge of an independent break-through to literate civilization. This marvellous perspective of mankind had been wrecked and plundered by European invaders; it was a human obligation to find and preserve what still existed. And indeed the collectors followed hard on the heels of the pioneers and of the vanishing Indian cultures. In the first place, scrupulous credit must be given to the great collectors of languages and objects: the Federal Bureau of American Ethnology, the Smithsonian, the New York Museum of Natural History, Edward Ward Putnam at Harvard. But the story thereafter was more complex; George Herbert Mead and Benjamin Lee Whorf were in many ways profoundly American, but Franz Boas and Edward Sapir were both Jewish and both German, though they learned their trade in America and made their first intellectual impact there. And then one must bring into account the Freudian immigration and the diverse Freudian influences of the 1920s and 1930s.

There is general agreement that the landmarks were Margaret Mead's first two books, *Coming of Age in Samoa* (1928)[2] and *Growing up in New Guinea* (1930),[3] and Ruth Benedict's *Patterns of Culture* (1934).[4]

There were other good monographs, less widely sold, and it is almost true to say that good work came first, reflection later. The influences that then flowed in provoked very sophisticated debate, much more elaborate field work, and perhaps in the end frustration.[5]

I do not think the cultural anthropologists used the word 'identity' in a technical sense until Erikson made it popular: but perhaps it is fair to foist it on them, in the context of this discussion, because one of their primary methodological assumptions was that a culture was unique, consistent and binding. These were similar in scope to the assumptions of structural

2. Jonathan Cape, 1929; Penguin Books, 1943.
3. Routledge & Sons, 1931; Penguin Books, 1942.
4. Routledge & Kegan Paul, 1935.
5. See for example a social anthropologist's view of 'The Rise and Fall of Culture and Personality': Hilary Callan, *Ethnology & Society* (Clarendon Press, 1970), p. 7.

anthropology, that savages are not fools, that their institutions have passed the test of 'fitness to the environment', and that we should watch, listen and understand before we criticize. But they were not the same, and yet it is not very easy to specify the differences. Perhaps the paradigm of functional anthropology is that of a biological 'system', to be understood not of course as a machine but as a physiological 'creature'. Perhaps the paradigm of culture is language (I am thinking here of the influence of Sapir and Whorf).[6] One is bound to say that the working of language is still very imperfectly understood, but it obviously has these characteristics, that within a group it is unique, consistent, and binding. Indeed, it would be reasonable enough to reverse the argument, and to define a group and its boundaries in terms of a language which is unique, consistent and binding.

What is more, the analogy of language can be pursued into the discussion of style; the style of a culture, as of any given period in art, is unique and pervasive. The insight is helpful, yet the analogy is easy to kick to pieces. Of what use is the analogy of language when we do not understand language? In the old tag, this is to explain *obscurum per obscurius*, to explain a puzzle by offering an even harder puzzle. A language faces the same puzzles as a culture. How is it learnt? what range of deviation does it permit? what are its boundaries? how is it sustained? how is it changed?

In consequence, there are problems of definition, of method, of underlying or inarticulate philosophy.[7]

Here are two examples of definitions of a quite practical kind.

A culture is the way of life of a group of people, the configuration of all of the more or less stereotyped patterns of learned behavior which are handed down from one generation to the next through the means of language and imitation.   (p. 5)

6. For some references see 'The Sapir-Whorf Hypothesis', in Barnouw (1963), pp. 95–9.

7. I have drawn mainly on Victor Barnouw, *Culture and Personality* (Dorsey Press, Homewood, Ill., 1963) and on various works of Clyde Kluckhohn, in particular *Culture and Behavior*, ed. Richard Kluckhohn, (Free Press, New York, 1962).

Personality is a more or less enduring organization of forces within the individual associated with a complex of fairly consistent attitudes, values, and modes of perception which account, in part, for the individual's consistency of behavior.   (p. 8)

These are 'word/thing' definitions in the sense that they postulate an existent 'thing' and tag it with a word. But the definitions are vague (each includes 'more or less' – how much more and how much less ?) and include difficult terms such as 'language', and 'attitudes, values and modes of perception'. And what sort of 'things' are these, and need we postulate them ? One might perhaps shift the focus from observed to observer and treat these not as 'things' but as 'constructs'. 'Psychology called its causal construct "personality" and anthropology called its construct "culture"' (Richard Kluckhohn in his introduction to *Culture and Behavior*, 1962, p. 8). This is quite plausible; in one sense 'another person' is to me a set of my generalizations which give me rules for prediction and corresponding action in relation to an external object with which I am in some way involved. In the Gospel the blind man who regained his sight saw men at first as 'trees walking';[8] a hypothesis to be tested by further experience. But in that case, how do we guarantee interpersonal consistency between the constructs of different observers ?

Hence a second set of problems, those about method. There are plenty of quotable cases in which a second observer directly challenged a first observer's findings about the character of a culture and about the range of permissible differences within it, of 'permissible identities'. To meet this, one must have recourse to measurement, and one moves into the enormous field of personality tests and attitude surveys. It would be ridiculous to write all this off as a dead loss; but it produces much duller, less 'insightful' books than those of the pioneers, and there are of course conceptual difficulties. Take for instance Rorschach blots, which Barnouw discusses interestingly and at some length.[9] The problem is to settle whether individual imaginative responses do or do not differ as between cultures. The test lies

8. *St Mark*, viii, 24.
9. Chapter 15, pp. 239–59.

in the judgement of skilled Rorschach interpreters: but each interpreter is trained in one culture, and not in both, and it is hard to see quite how a logically adequate tester is to be trained and tested. Similarly with cross-cultural studies of attitudes of the kind used by Almond and Verba,[10] who used an expensive combination of sample survey and attitude questionnaires to compare and classify the political cultures of the U.S.A., the U.K., Western Germany, Italy and Mexico. Sophisticated regression analysis can draw attention to oddities in the data, but it cannot amend them or 'explain' them. There remains a field open to imaginative literary insight.

But this runs into the third kind of opposition, which treats with suspicion any statement which claims to be based on individual insight not further checked or analysed. In one form, this attack denies the status of 'knowledge' to any form of personal insight not refutable at least in principle. This does not deny the validity of imagination, it merely notes that, for example, the early work of Margaret Mead is no more 'knowledge' than is *Paradise Lost* or a Mozart piano sonata. In another form it postulates 'cultural relativism', and claims that there is no such thing as 'person' outside 'culture', that the psychoanalyst himself or herself speaks from within a culture and has insight only within a given social situation, that there are no generalizations possible about 'man *qua* man' except physiological ones. This runs parallel to an attack on implied determinism, an implication which is about equally distasteful to some Marxists, some Christians, and some free-thinking liberals.

And so on. But one principal reason for the general disrepute of cultural anthropology in recent years is similar to that which has embarrassed general theories of political development; that national resources were deployed to make an intellectual skill into an agency of national policy.

The first well-known example is Ruth Benedict's very sensitive study of Japanese culture, *The Chrysanthemum and the Sword*,[11] written when she was working for the Office of War

10. *The Civic Culture* (Princeton University Press, 1963).
11. Houghton Mifflin, Boston, 1946.

Information in Washington. Ruth Benedict had never visited Japan and claims only a superficial knowledge of Japanese. But she read very widely about Japan, made herself intimately familiar with Japanese artefacts, and interviewed Japanese in America, both Issei and Nisei, i.e. Japanese-born and born in America. The book was very influential, both among the American public and specifically during the American occupation of Japan; and one is bound to say that it was a 'good' book, in two senses, as a work of art and as an influence towards gentleness and patience in dealing with an alien and conquered enemy. But the Pacific War passed over into the Cold War, which tended at that time to assume a world-wide character, as a war against Communism rather than against Russia. Hence a group of studies by different authors, published in the early 1950s – and perhaps many more still lie buried in the Washington archives. Many of the published studies were reviewed together by Clyde Kluckhohn in 1955,[12] more or less at the end of this phase, and it is interesting that one can include here two political scientists influential in the next phase, that of studies in political development. These were Gabriel Almond, whose first important work, *The Appeals of Communism*, was published in 1954;[13] and Lucian Pye, whose book on *Guerrilla Communism in Malaya* (1956) was discussed earlier (Chap. 3). This group might also include Nathan Leites's books *The Operational Code of the Politburo* (1951)[14] and *A Study of Bolshevism*,[15] published in 1953, and his book with Elsa Bemant, *Ritual of Liquidation: The Case of the Moscow Trials*,[16] published in 1954. But it was in particular the work of Geoffrey Gorer (one of the few British cultural anthropologists) on *The People of Great Russia*[17] which caused a sceptical raising of eyebrows. To quote the survey by

12. An article on 'Recent studies of the "national character" of Great Russians': reprinted in Kluckhohn, 1962. There are also books by Margaret Mead; *Soviet Attitudes toward Authority* (McGraw-Hill, New York, 1951; Tavistock Publications Ltd, London, 1955) and (with Rhoda Metraux) *The Study of Culture at a Distance* (Chicago University Press, 1953).

13. Princeton University Press.   14. McGraw-Hill, New York.

15. Free Press, New York.   16. Free Press, New York.

17. With J. Rickman, Cresset Press, 1949.

Kluckhohn, 'That he is guilty of loose statements, unwarranted assumptions, dubious analogies, and factual errors is unarguable . . . And it cannot be emphasized too strongly that the reader hardly ever knows where he stands on evidential grounds.' In this case, it did not help that the book was well written. Indeed, this helped to discredit it, in a period when 'behavioral scientists' were sharpening their hatchets methodologically, because it stood out plainly as a readable account of what used to be called 'national character', in the days before social science was invented. Even then, the 'national character' approach to history had become something of a joke, discredited alike by trained professional historians and by Marxism. Here it was again, in a crude form, in a more sceptical age, and it risked being condemned out of hand.[18]

Popular success, academic failure, were confirmed because of the 'swaddling hypothesis'. Russian peasant children used, for their first months, to be 'swaddled' in the old sense, which one can see in some late medieval pictures; that is to say, bandaged tightly and bound to a board. There are many 'folk lore' arguments about this: that it helps to straighten the child's back, that it prevents it scratching itself, that it guarantees that it will not suffer frost-bite in a Russian winter. But it was extremely remote from the America of Dr Spock: the child free to kick on the hearth rug, to choose when to eat, when to sleep: and Russian witnesses in exile were rather embarrassed and evasive about it. Child psychologists (including Erikson) did not reject the possibility that differences of child-rearing practice might affect character. But of course the argument is circular; differences of 'character' or culture would influence child-rearing practices and would also influence children in many other ways. And Gorer seemed to be committed to a strong theory of 'childhood determinism',[19] as regards personality and culture, which was

18. Especially as he did it also to the English: *Exploring English Character: A Study of the Morals and Behavior of the English People* (Criterion, New York, 1955).

19. He is discussed under this heading in Barnouw's book: Chapter Eight, 'Childhood Determinism and the Study of National Character', pp. 120–36.

really not tenable at all, except in a much weaker form. And there was complete confusion about the exact nature of swaddling practices, about the range of variation within Russia, about the rate of obsolescence of old peasant customs. This association with popularization and with Cold War politics certainly damaged the intellectual reputation of cultural anthropology. It also enforced the necessity of disciplined technical development in the field of personality and culture, and Barnouw's book, published in 1963, is mainly concerned with attempts to measure interactions between individual and culture. This produces what (I fear) is common experience: that an 'insight' is put through the drill of 'research' and emerges from it (as it were) filleted, or ground small. The verdict is that there is something in it, but that there are many other factors, and also that our research tools measure only to limited degrees of significance.

It was during this period of the later 1950s that studies of personality and culture made their impact on political science. This happened on a broad front at the time when academic prestige and intellectual curiosity both demanded the revival of comparative study. Here was one comparative discipline ready to hand. It also happened on a narrower front, in that a key point was that of 'socialization into a culture'. How were children socialized into different political cultures?[20] It was an obvious question, but a hard one; made even harder by the growing recognition of the existence (in a 'great society') of sub-cultures, including linguistic sub-cultures.[21] 'Cultural anthropology'

20. There is a useful survey by Dennis Kavanagh, *Political Culture* (Macmillan, 1972), and some influential books about children – Herbert Hyman, *Political Socialization: A Study in the Psychology of Political Behavior* (Free Press, New York, 1959); Fred I. Greenstein, *Children and Politics* (1965; revised ed., Yale University Press, 1969): D. Easton and J. Dennis, *Children in the Political System: Origins of Political Legitimacy* (McGraw-Hill, New York, 1969): Dean Jaros, *Socialization to Politics* (Nelson, 1973); Ted Tapper, *Young People & Society* (Faber & Faber, 1971); see also R. E. Dowse's review article, 'Psychology and Politics', *Political Studies*, 18, 1970, p. 408, and other articles by him.

21. See P. P. Giglioli (ed.), *Language and Social Context* (Penguin, 1973); in particular the articles of B. Bernstein and W. Labov.

played an important part in stating the central problems of social identity, of 'I' and 'we', 'us' and 'them'. But it has not resolved them, and has perhaps exhausted the possibilities open to it within its original terms of reference as a separate technique or discipline.

Part Two
WORD AND CONCEPT

Words are the tokens current and accepted for con-
ceits, as moneys are for values.

BACON, *Advancement of Learning*, Bk I, xvi, 3.

So far, it has been possible to play the 'whodunnit' game with
some confidence. Lucian Pye invented the phrase 'political
identity' in or about 1960; he deliberately adapted it from the
usage of Erik Erikson, who began to write about the crises of
'personal identity' in or about 1946. Erikson in turn acknowledges two lines of descent in the development of his ideas;
one of them from Freud and the Freudians, the other from the
native American school of personality and culture. Both cultural
anthropology and the comparative study of political culture ran
into difficulties and are held to have discredited themselves,
because of their alliance with American national policy in the
1950s and 1960s.

What was discreditable about that ? A social scientist is told to
regard himself as a servant of humanity, not of a particular
political agent. But a social scientist cannot pursue his avocation
without social support, expressed in terms of social access and
approval, and indeed in the more vulgar form of financial
support.[1] Furthermore, a social scientist is not free from social
ties and social vanities. If people say 'come down out of your
ivory tower and lend a hand', he or she responds morally and
does what he or she can. There is no reason to scatter allegations
of hypocrisy.

But the real temptation is rather different; it lies in the fact
that involvement entails commitment, and that commitment
strains the bonds of scientific austerity. Political culture and

1. See, for instance, my article, 'The Conceptual Framework and the
Cash Basis' (1958; reprinted in *Explorations in Government* [Macmillan,
1975], p. 301).

political identity became part of the everyday language of politics; their academic sponsors were involved in the eddying stream of political events (as Donal Cruise O'Brien's article illustrates so well);[2] and then the academic criticisms of other academics began to bite.

So farewell to the Gurus of yesteryear.

Yet this tidy and banal conclusion ('Whose social scientist are you?') left me dissatisfied. The hunt after the word 'identity' led to Ruth Benedict's sentence which I have put at the head of Chapter Five: 'There is no proper antagonism between the role of society and that of the individual.' At first sight the sentence is so transparent as to seem self-evident; on reflection, no single word in it is unambiguous, and yet the statement seems important, leads one on to seek clarification.

At this point, I realized that I was moving from word to concept; and that there were difficult conceptual questions, for which the word 'identity' (whether personal, or political and social) might prove as good a label as any other.

I was thus led to go one move further back. Erikson's work and his life experience pointed both to an American native tradition and to a European tradition. The latter reached the United States through various channels, and was not uniform in its impact or in its teaching. In politics, for instance, I might have taken up instead the teaching of Karl Joachim Friedrich or of Arnold Brecht. But the case of the Frankfurt School is particularly challenging, because of the extraordinary personal impact of some of its members, in particular Fromm and Marcuse; and there has recently been a good book about it.[3]

French political philosophy had no similar impact in America (except perhaps through Sartre's plays) because there were virtually no French academic exiles; but in a European balance, French thought weighs at least as heavily as does German thought. Indeed, European thought about human identity involves an interplay of two languages; of German in the

2. Above p. 32, fn. 5.
3. Martin Jay, *The Dialectical Imagination, A History of the Frankfurt School and the Institute of Social Research, 1923–50* (Heinemann, 1973).

philosophers Kant, Hegel, Marx and Freud, of French in the novelists and poets – Stendhal, Balzac, Flaubert, Proust, Baudelaire, Rimbaud. Merely to indicate that theme is to show that it cannot be handled here. But my concern with it grew step by step out of a somewhat pedantic joke about the misuse of a phrase.

The same concern with usage led me also towards Erving Goffman. The Europeans make little use of the word 'identity' or its kindred in this sense, though it may perhaps find its way back into French and German from the U.S.A. In English it has been firmly implanted not only by the vogue for political culture, but also by the vogue for Goffman. His problem, I believe, is conceptually the same: but his tactics are determined partly by his wariness in avoiding the pits into which others have fallen. More of this in Chapter 8; the upshot is that he seems detached from the main stream of thought, and yet has become indispensable to it, a separate American voice, another shaper of analytic idiom.

CHAPTER 6

ALIENATION AND IDENTITY

Ich ist in der Welt zu Hause, wenn es sie kennt, noch
mehr, wenn es sie begriffen hat.

HEGEL : *Philosophie des Rechts* (Glockner ed., Vol.
7, para. 4, additions).[1]

I HAD begun this study before I knew of Richard Schacht's book
on *Alienation*,[2] published in 1971, in which he has done similar
work, in a more professional way, on a related word or concept.
Alienation, he says, has become a 'fetish word'. To quote a
reviewer, ' "Alienation" is in danger of becoming one of these
comfortable words which smoothly obscure the states of mind
they label.'[3] So with 'identity'. But that word does not appear in
Schacht's index,[4] and the words seem to have been 'twinned'
first by Erich Fromm. This is clear in *The Fear of Freedom*, first
published in England in 1942, and it may be that if one worked
through their early works one would find that Fromm has
priority over Erikson in developing the present use of the word
'identity'.

The two men have had parallel careers and similar interests,
yet their doctrines and influence can be placed in contrast. Like
Erikson, Fromm was born just too late to fight in the First
World War, and grew up in Central Europe 'between the wars'.
Like him, he was trained in psychoanalysis (but in Berlin, not in

1. The key words in this ('*Ich*', '*Welt*', '*zu Hause*', '*kennt*', '*begriffen*') had
been given a technical sense by Hegel, and translators disagree. Perhaps –
the 'I' is at home in the world, if it has become acquainted with it; still more
so if it has formed a concept of it.
2. Allen & Unwin.
3. A. S. Byatt, *The Times*, 19 August 1971. Compare the phrase in Walter
Kaufmann's Introductory Essay to Richard Schacht's book: 'bargain words
that cost little or no study and can be used in a great variety of contexts with
an air of expertise' (p. xlviii).
4. But see Chapter 9.1, fn. 4.

Vienna) without medical qualifications. Like him, he was exiled to America in the 1930s, and became a best-seller there.

One profound difference was that Fromm is Jewish and has found part of his own 'identity' in the Jewish tradition, though he ceased long ago to be a practising Jew. Some of his most original and appealing work places Moses alongside Marx and Freud, in order to illustrate Messianic theories of history (by no means the same as Utopias).[5] But it is more relevant in the present context that he was for some twenty-five years a leading member of the 'Frankfurt School' both in Germany and in exile in the U.S.A. There is an excellent history by Martin Jay,[6] who tells in detail the story of its founders and adherents, its splits and deviations; and one way to specify its influence on social thought is simply to take his bibliographical list of those associated with it and to put the best known names in alphabetical order: T. W. Adorno, Walter Benjamin, Bruno Bettelheim, Franz Borkenau, Erich Fromm, Max Horkheimer, Marie Jahoda, Morris Janowitz, Otto Kirchheimer, Paul Lazarsfeld, Herbert Marcuse, Franz Neumann, Karl Wittfogel. These were diverse people, who came and went; the central figures have been Horkheimer and Adorno, and now Habermas in the School restored to post-war Germany, and it is perhaps from these three that one must attempt to generalize.

They were largely Jewish, the brilliant sons of successful middle-class families: but (except for Fromm) they placed themselves in a European tradition, not in a Jewish one. They sought to link Freud and Marx, paying great honour to both men; but the school bred dissident Freudians and dissident Marxists. In particular, they were among the early students of 'young Marx', were hostile to Stalinism, lacked enthusiasm for dogmatic Leninism. They would not have made good Bolsheviks, because dogmatism and bureaucracy were their enemies and they sought

---

5. Cf. *The Sane Society*, pp. 121–3, and see references in the index under Religion Jewish, Religion Mosaic, Tradition Judaeo-Christian.
6. Above, p. 50, fn 3. See also Lazarsfeld's reflections, in his article on 'Sociology' in *Main Trends of Research in the Social and Human Sciences. Part One: Social Sciences* (Mouton/UNESCO, 1970), pp. 111–17.

to sustain the tradition of 'critical' philosophy. There were among them several gifted musicians, and they gave a high place to the historical and philosophical study of music, art and literature.[7] In Germany, their preferred method was historical rather than (in a positivist sense) empirical, and some of them were perhaps a little contemptuous of the American style in social science. But some (for instance, Adorno and Lazarsfeld) learnt statistical method and had great influence on its development in psychology and in political science.

This was not the only group of exiles to influence American thought; there were other 'humanist' groups, and perhaps the natural scientists had more influence on events than all these groups together.[8] But the School has historically a special place in that it introduced 'critical Marxism' to the American academic world. They were wisely cautious in avoiding a head-on clash with American prejudices about Communism. But they kept the study of Marx honourably alive even in the harshest times; and their tradition had an extraordinary late flowering in the vogue for Herbert Marcuse, who became in his late sixties one of the gurus of the student revolution.[9]

Their Marxism, however, excluded them from the main stream of American thought about political development, so that ideas about the crisis of identity flowed into it through Erikson primarily. Note that Erikson was not anti-Marxist; he was simply non-Marxist, and virtually free from Hegelian or Marxist terminology. 'Alienation' is not one of his words.

I. FROMM

We communicate, but being abstract and second-hand, the modes of our communication do not achieve community.

7. Georg Lukács went his own way, but belonged to the same 'tendency'; one reason for his difficult relations with Soviet authorities.
8. See for instance D. Fleming and B. Bailyn (eds.), *The Intellectual Migration: Europe and America, 1930–1960*, Harvard University Press, 1969; and Robert Berger (ed.), *The Legacy of German Refugee Intellectuals* (New York, 1922).
9. He was born in 1898, died in 1974.

George Steiner, *Language & Silence* (Faber & Faber, 1967), p. 231.

It would be revealing to make a comparative analysis of the Freudian and Neo-Freudian styles. The latter, in the more philosophical writings, frequently comes close to that of the sermon, or of the social worker; it is elevated and yet clear, permeated with goodwill and tolerance and yet moved by an *esprit de sérieux* which makes transcendental values into facts of everyday life. What has become a sham is taken as real. In contrast, there is a strong undertone of irony in Freud's usage of 'freedom', 'happiness', 'personality'; either these terms seem to have invisible quotation marks, or their negative content is explicitly stated.

Herbert Marcuse, *Eros and Civilization* (1955; Sphere Books, 1969, p. 204).

I must confess that Erich Fromm (who is still alive and active)[10] remains for me elusive and impersonal. Perhaps this is partly because of the character of his prose style. The inner group of the Frankfurt School never lost in the U.S.A. their dream of civilizing Germany, or of bringing it back to its true self. They were fluent in English but thought in German; George Steiner in discussing translation refers to 'the German form with its endless spiralling sentences, mass of composite words and emphatic substantives through which Broch tries to express a simultaneity of physical and metaphysical meanings'.[11] As will be seen in Part III, I conceptualize political identity largely in terms of inter-personal language and its 'rhetoric'; perhaps my ear, brought up in a confusion of English, Scottish, American, Irish voices, is neurotically sensitive, or even 'racialist', about vocal images. In a sense, the rough (not 'broken') English of the Central Europeans did them honour; they never ceased to assert their identity in exile, and some of them returned and renewed the battle for what they saw as the true German philosophy. It will be some time yet before it is possible to strike a balance of profit and loss for 'the Battle over Positivism in

10. *The Anatomy of Human Destructiveness* (Jonathan Cape, 1974).
11. *After Babel* (Oxford University Press, 1975), p. 320.

German Sociology', to which Adorno committed his last years.[12]

I refer again to this problem of language in discussing Marcuse (below pp. 66, 67). They both write in Anglo-German, and this is one reason why they are difficult to summarize and to pin down. The linguistic entities which haunt them are slightly alien to us even as translated, and we are apt to react with antipathy without adequate reflection. This at any rate, is the only defence I can find for Fromm, in face of the charge documented up to the hilt in Schacht's book, that Fromm is radically inconsistent in the use of terms essential to his teaching: in particular, 'alienation', 'nature', 'individual identity'. The truth may be that such words have an essential unity in German yet penetrate into the English language only in a diffuse, prismatic, refracted form. It is possible, too, that Fromm's teaching is better adapted to a direct interchange with individual patients in the course of therapy; and of course for that purpose consistency in the use of words is no great virtue. 'In lapidary inscriptions a man is not upon oath,' said Dr Johnson. Nor is he when acting as confessor; and Fromm became very popular as confessor-general to Americans of his generation, partly because he persuasively blackened their sins, and then gave absolution.

Nevertheless, I think there are fixed points.

One of them is that he never moves far from the spirit of 'young Karl Marx' as he understood it. This is his translation of a passage published in 1844 when Marx was about twenty-five.

Every one of your relationships to man and to nature must be a definite expression of your *real, individual* life corresponding to the object of your will. If you love without calling forth love, that is, if your love as such does not produce love, if by means of an *expression*

12. There is a valuable article by Gillian Rose in *Political Studies*, 24 (1976), pp. 69–85: 'How is Critical Theory Possible? Theodor W. Adorno and Concept Formation in Sociology'. It further confuses the present enquiry that Adorno has his own peculiar usage of 'identity': 'Identity Thinking', 'Non-Identity Thinking' and 'Rational Identity Thinking' (Rose, p. 70). See also Helmut Dubiel, *Identität und Institution: Studien über moderne Sozialphilosophien*, Bertelsmann, Düsseldorf, 1973).

of life as a loving person you do not make of yourself a *loved person*, then your love is impotent, a misfortune.[13]

(*S.S.*, p. 132)[14]

A second is that he operates with a very simple model of man and nature. Man's 'natural' condition is one of harmony with 'nature' and his fellow-man.

This identity with nature, clan, religion, gives the individual security. He belongs to, he is rooted in, a structuralized whole in which he has an unquestionable place. He may suffer from hunger or suppression, but he does not suffer from the worst of all pains – complete aloneness and doubt.

(*F.F.*, pp. 28–9)

But by man's own 'nature' he turns against 'nature', and finds himself alone.

The kind of relatedness to the world may be noble or trivial, but even being related to the basest kind of pattern is immensely preferable to being alone. Religion and nationalism, as well as any custom and any belief however absurd and degrading, if it only connects the individual with others, are refuges from what man most dreads: isolation.

(*F.F.*, p. 15)

There is another element, however, which makes the need to 'belong' so compelling: the fact of subjective self-consciousness, of the faculty of thinking by which man is aware of himself as an individual entity, different from nature and other people.

(*F.F.*, pp. 16–17)

If we call this organized and integrated whole of the personality the self, we can also say that the *one side of the growing process of individualism is the growth of self-strength*. The limits of the growth of individuation and the self are set, partly by individual conditions, but

13. 'Nationalökonomie und Philosophie', 1844, published in Karl Marx, *Die Frühschriften*, Alfred Kröner Verlag, Stüttgart, 1953, pp. 300, 301.
14. '*F.F*' stands for *The Fear of Freedom* (1942: Routledge & Kegan Paul, 1960); '*S.S.*' for *The Sane Society* (1956; Routledge & Kegan Paul, 1963).

essentially by social conditions. For although the differences between individuals in this respect appear to be great, every society is characterized by a certain level of individuation beyond which the normal individual cannot go.

(*F.F.*, p. 23)

In one sense this is a natural stage in the development of 'individual' personality.

The child becomes more free *to* develop and express its own individual self unhampered by those ties which were limiting it. But the child also becomes more free *from* a world which gave it security and reassurance. The process of individuation is one of growing strength and integration of its individual personality, but it is at the same time a process in which the original identity with others is lost and in which the child becomes more separate from them.

(*F.F.*, pp. 24–5)

But it is an unhappy stage, and the individual must fight his way out of 'alienation' so as to establish an identity. But this may in some sense be a false identity.

The loss of the self and its substitution by a pseudo-self leave the individual in an intense state of insecurity. He is obsessed by doubt since, being essentially a reflex of other people's expectation of him, he has in a measure lost his identity. In order to overcome the panic resulting from such loss of identity, he is compelled to conform, to seek his identity by continuous approval and recognition by others.

(*F.F.*, pp. 177–8)

The identity of the individual has been a major problem of modern philosophy since Descartes. Today we take for granted that we are we. Yet the doubt about ourselves still exists, or has even grown. In his plays Pirandello has given expression to this feeling of modern man. He starts with the question: Who am I? What proof have I for my own identity other than the continuation of my physical self? His answer is not like Descartes' – the affirmation of the individual self – but its denial: I have no identity, there is no self excepting the one which is the reflex of what others expect me to be: I am 'as you desire me'.

(*F.F.*, p. 219)

(Notice that on p. 177 of *F.F.* one has a clear case of the word 'identity' used to mean 'true self' or 'integrated personality'. But in the quotation from p. 219, the word still carries a strong flavour of seventeenth-century origins referred to in Chapter 2–2.

The Identity of the same Man consists . . . in nothing but a participation of the same continued Life, by constantly fleeting Particles of Matter, in succession vitally united to the same organized Body.)

Primitive man had no such difficulty.

The average man today obtains his sense of identity from his belonging to a nation, rather than from his being a 'son of man'.

(*S.S.*, p. 58)

The member of a primitive clan might express his sense of identity in the formula 'I am we'; he cannot yet conceive of himself as an 'individual', existing apart from his group.

(*S.S.*, p. 61)

Since I cannot remain sane without the sense of 'I', I am driven to do almost anything to acquire this sense. Behind the intense passion for status and conformity is this very need, and it is sometimes even stronger than the need for physical survival.

(*S.S.*, p. 63)

But the condition of man now is insecure and uncertain.

Free man is by necessity insecure; thinking man by necessity uncertain.
How, then, can man tolerate this insecurity inherent in human existence ? One way is to be rooted in the group in such a way that the feeling of identity is guaranteed by the membership of the group, be it family, clan, nation, class. As long as the process of individualism has not reached a stage where the individual emerges from these primary bonds, he is still 'we', and as long as the group functions he is certain of his own identity by his membership in it.

(*S.S.*, pp. 196–7)

There is no escape except through 'success'.

Indeed, with the experience of self disappears the experience of identity – and when this happens, man could become insane if he did not save himself by acquiring a *secondary sense of self*; he does that by experiencing himself as being approved of, worth while, successful, useful – briefly, as a saleable commodity which is *he* because he is looked upon by others as an entity, not unique but fitting into one of the current patterns.

(*S.S.*, p. 143)

And success may still be alienation. 'What is a man profited, if he shall gain the whole world, and lose his own soul ?'[15]

This model, I suppose, could perhaps (with some strain) be called Hegelian, and it is couched in such vague and general terms that it can hardly be called Freudian at all.

And (this is the third point) it is Marxist only in a very limited sense. In the later Marx alienation is closely associated with work; the dialectic of productive forces has created under capitalism a situation in which a man's work is not 'his own', is alienated from him. Alienation is social, not individual; it can be cured only by radical social change, and such change requires revolutionary spirit and (probably) revolutionary violence. For Fromm, this quotation is typical:

Man today is confronted with the most fundamental choice; not that between Capitalism or Communism, but that between *robotism* (of both the Capitalist and the Communist variety), or Humanistic Communitarian Socialism. Most facts seem to indicate that he is choosing robotism, and that means, in the long run, insanity and destruction. But all these facts are not strong enough to destroy faith in man's reason, good will and sanity.

(*S.S.*, p. 363)

He blames not only man's eternal nature: but also a specific form of organization, and he prescribes an organizational remedy. He ends, in fact, as a nineteenth-century Utopian, not as an advocate of revolutionary action.

Fear of Freedom has been reprinted many times, and has been prescribed reading for any debate about the modern doctrines of individual and social identity. But I am afraid it must be judged rhetoric, a culinary confection to suit all tastes, rather than as a work of science and philosophy. There is of course much more in it than can be summarized here; but who could dissent from

15. Matthew, xvi, 26.

Fromm on these three points – love, individuality and social conditions of work? He is like the proverbial preacher who preached on Sin; the congregation gathered that he was against it.

2. MARCUSE

And it shall come to pass afterward, that I will pour out my Spirit upon all flesh; and your sons and your daughters shall prophesy, your old men shall dream dreams, your young men shall see visions . . .

And I will show wonders in the heavens and in the earth, blood, and fire, and pillars of smoke.

The sun shall be turned into darkness, and the moon into blood, before the great and the terrible day of the Lord come.

Joel II, 28, 30, 31

Herbert Marcuse died in 1974 at the age of seventy-six. He had been a scholar in the critical tradition of Frankfurt for some fifty years, was known to scholars as a pioneer in the study of 'young Hegel' and 'young Marx' and was reckoned respectable enough by the American military and academic establishment to hold a post as research worker in O.S.S. (the Office of Strategic Services, the forerunner of the C.I.A.) and then a series of professorships in good American universities in the 1950s and 1960s.

Then in his late sixties he became the grandfather-figure of the American and international student revolution, perhaps the only hard and serious scholar that it possessed, and its only international man.

The quotation that heads this chapter is therefore irresistible: but is it appropriate? That would be a good question if we had the material with which to answer it. Here I react strongly, but mainly on instinct, against the present fashion for deriding Marcuse and with him the student movement.

I never had the luck to see and listen to Marcuse in his days of fame, but certainly he had neither the manner nor the style of the Old Testament. Nor did he have the manner and style of the stage-managed modern prophet. He was not (so far as one could discern) on pilgrimage to promote the sale of his books (which did sell enormously in paperback, hard though they are to read). Nor did he owe allegiance (so far as one could discern) to any front organization, sect, or *groupuscule*; he was in a sense a theologian himself, but (so far, at least) there has been no theological struggle among disciples to divide his raiment and claim inheritance.

Marcuse spoke from within a long philosophical tradition, and he made that tradition into a way of life, in the sense that all he wrote and said was related to and continually modifies and re-adapts a complex system of ideas – and (Marxist though he is) the theme is 'ideas', not 'words' nor 'things'.

For most of his life he spoke and wrote out of season. Then it turned out that what he had written in the 1930s, 1940s, 1950s, with no great public acclaim, clicked (like the combination of a safe) into the mood of radicalism in the 1960s, culminating in the odd happenings of 1968. He is (to my mind) the best theorist of these happenings, in what he wrote long before, envisaging no such sequel.

Inevitably, discussion of Marcuse has been concerned in the first instance with the lectures and essays of his old age, when his name was known in all the universities of the world. These include some foolish things, and critics have answered them according to their folly – as the author of *Proverbs* ambiguously advised.[16] At least, he observed the wisdom of Dylan Thomas:

> Do not go gentle into that good night.
> Old age should burn and rave at close of day;
> Rage, rage against the dying of the light.[17]

16. Answer not a fool according to his folly,
  lest thou also be like unto him.
  Answer a fool according to his folly, lest he be
  wise in his own conceit.
  Proverbs, XXVI, 4, 5.
Among these critics are: A. MacIntyre, *Marcuse* (Fontana–Collins, 1970), M. Cranston, 'Herbert Marcuse' (*Encounter* 32 [1969] p. 39, and in *The New Left*, ed. Cranston [Bodley Head, 1970]; Martin Seliger, 'Locke and Marcuse – Intermittent and Millennial Revolutionism' in *Festschrift für Karl Loewenstein* (Mohr, Tübingen, 1971), p. 427.
17. *Collected Poems 1934–1952* (Dent, 1952), p. 116.

And he had earned this easing of his rage by a life devoted to scholarship, which at the end could be seen to sum up four main concerns, each of major significance.

In the 1920s Marcuse was perhaps primarily a student of imaginative literature, finding the driving force of German thought in poets rather than in philosophers; and above all in Schiller, whose *Letters on the Aesthetic Education of Man* (1795) 'aim at a remaking of civilization by virtue of the liberating force of the aesthetic function'.[18] An English reader will think at once of Shelley's *A Defence of Poetry* (1821):[19] 'all high poetry is infinite; it is as the first acorn, which contained all oaks potentially'. This is a theme which is alive in Marcuse to the end: one of his last essays, flawed but interesting, is on 'Art and Revolution'.[20]

His second life-work was that of a professional student of German philosophy in the critical tradition. Nothing could be more traditional and stilted than the title of the thesis, approved in 1932, which qualified him to hold a professorial chair in a German university: *Hegels Ontologie und die Grundlegung einer Theorie der Geschichtlichkeit* – 'Hegel's Doctrine of Being and the Basis of a Theory of Historicity'.[21] Pedantic this may have been in style, as the etiquette of the Habilitationsschrift prescribed; and it was unquestionably learned. But there underlay it a view of Hegel and of the nature of philosophy which became part of his character. Dilthey had published a book on 'young Hegel' in 1921; Lukács followed in 1948. But perhaps Marcuse was the first to perceive Hegel as an imaginative and persistent critic, to

---

18. *Eros & Civilization* (1955; Sphere Books, 1969) p. 148. In Glasgow University Library there is a copy of Marcuse's bibliography of Schiller, published in Berlin in 1925. But the bibliography of Marcuse's work, appended to the *Festschrift* edited by K. H. Wolff and Barrington Moore (*The Critical Spirit*, Beacon Press, Boston, 1967), indicates that he never followed that theme directly.

19. Conveniently available in *Shelley: Political Writings* (R. A. Duerkson, ed., Appleton Century, New York, 1970), p. 187.

20. Chapter 3 of *Counterrevolution and Revolt* (Allen Lane, 1972).

21. Frankfurt am Main, 1925. I have not seen a copy of this, and I do not think it has been translated.

answer in advance, as it were, the attack made by Popper in *The Open Society and its Enemies*, published in 1945, and also in *The Poverty of Historicism* (1957).[22] MacIntyre writes, rather scornfully, that Marcuse became and remained a Young Hegelian of the 1840s.[23] He was also one of the first to comment, in 1932, on the publication of Marx's *Economic and Philosophical Manuscripts of 1844*,[24] and it is in a sense true that he remained for all his life immersed in the conceptual problems of that important decade. Certainly, he did not feel, as did the older Marx, that it was necessary to his 'science' to absorb and explore the economic 'science' of the English school. He remains contemptuous of positivism and operationalism in social science, ill-informed about their rôle in natural science. Marxist he must be called, since there is no Marxist pope or council to declare him heretical, and it is an open question what Marx meant by 'dialectics' and by 'materialism'.[25] Young Marcuse is strongly dialectical, strongly historical, strongly critical, but surely he is in a philosophical sense idealist and not materialist.

During this period Marcuse developed some connection with the Frankfurt School; he became one of their group in exile when he moved to the U.S.A. in 1934, and was a regular contributor to their journal, the *Zeitschrift für Sozialforschung*. Indeed, he also contributed an article on the history of ideas to their grandiose studies of *Authority and Family*: but this collaboration only emphasizes that at that stage he was very little concerned with their project of marrying Freud to Marx, depth studies of individual personality to depth studies of revolution.

His first substantial publication in English was a summing up of his work on Young Hegel and Young Marx, as he saw them in the historical context of the nineteenth century: *Reason and*

22. See 'Karl Popper and the Problem of Historical Laws' (1959), republished in *Studies in Critical Philosophy* (New Left Books, 1972).
23. MacIntyre, 1970, p. 22.
24. 'The Foundations of Historical Materialism', in *Studies in Critical Philosophy*, p. 3.
25. Paul Thomas, in 'Marx and Science' (*Political Studies* 24 [1976], p. 2, denies that Marx himself ever used the combined phrase, 'dialectical materialism'.

Revolution, published in 1941. There is much in it that can be challenged by later writers: but it is certainly a work of scholarship and imagination. I learnt much from it about an alien but powerful tradition of philosophy; and in particular about the problem of putting German philosophy into English words. Marcuse noted in the Preface his gratitude to 'Mr Edward M. David who gave the book the stylistic form it now has' (p. viii), so presumably it was drafted by Marcuse largely in German. The text seems to me more perspicuous than much of what Marcuse himself wrote later in English, and it does imply (between the lines) a running discussion about problems of philosophical translation. The jokes (in MacIntyre, for instance) about never using a four-letter word if an eighteen-letter word will do are quite misplaced. A poor German scholar (as I am) has no real difficulty with long German compound words, provided he knows the context. I picked up the phrase 'Kommentarunbedürftigkeit (twenty-four letters) des Kunstwerks' recently in a publisher's advertisement: it goes easily into English (in the same text) as 'the thought that a work of art needs no commentary' (ten words for three, forty-one letters for thirty-seven). But the small German words are diabolically hard, especially if they derive their contexts from the traditions of German philosophy. Try, for instance, *Wesen, Sein, Dasein, Seiende; Schein, Sinn, Sinnichkeit; Geist, Seele, Ding; Sicherinnern; Wert* and its derivatives, such as *Umwertung, Entwertung, Verwertung;* and so on. They look as if there should be simple Anglo-Saxon equivalents, but these will do only at a colloquial level. In philosophy, and indeed in any sophisticated discourse, the words are intelligible only within a tradition; perhaps this contributes to the general trend of German philosophy towards the study of 'wholes', and its distrust (except in Vienna and in Wittgenstein) of truth understood as a list of atomic propositions.

The result is that a translator is put to various shifts. Clearly Mr David advised that *Begriff* should be translated 'Notion'; he might just as well have left the word in German, as the word 'Notion' has in normal English use some strange senses quite unrelated to any of the meanings of *Begriff. Arbeit* is troublesome too; but worst of all are the usages of the various German words which appear in the context of 'alienation'.[26] Marcuse when he came to America was familiar with Greek, Latin and French as well as German. He acquired English to the point of being effectively bilingual, though he was never quite at home in English stylistically, as were Erikson, Polanyi, and Schrödinger, to whom I referred earlier. In his next phase or avatar he clearly mastered Russian to the point of being absorbed in the most rebarbative of Russian-language materials, the texts of official Soviet Marxism. This period ran from his recruitment to the State Department (or O.S.S. – it really does not matter which) in about 1940 to his move in 1957 from Harvard to Brandeis, which set him free, at the age of sixty, to resume his career as critical philosopher.

The book on *Soviet Marxism: A Critical Analysis*[27] eventually published in 1958, is quite unlike his other works in intellectual flavour. A friendly critic writes of its 'strangely academic and bloodless character',[28] and that is fair to its surface texture. But it also gives an impression of deep repressions and strains, to which Marcuse never gave full expression. One can suppose, imaginatively, that there was stress in three dimensions; first, through the political concerns of an exile compelled to play a non-political role in a period of violent oscillations of power; secondly, as an exile known to be a Marxist earning his living in public positions in the U.S.A. in the age of Senator Joe McCarthy; and, thirdly, as an intellectual striving to think coldly on a matter which involved a philosophic tradition which was dear to him. The book is sub-titled 'a critical analysis'; the word 'critical' reaffirms his creed, and asserts that he intends to write as a philosophic critic, not as sociologist, not as political analyst, not as a servant of United States policy.

The introduction begins thus:

This study attempts to evaluate some main trends of Soviet

26. I refer again to Richard Schacht's important book (p. 154 above).
27. (Columbia University Press, Routledge & Kegan Paul, 1958).
28. Paul A. Robinson, *The Sexual Radicals; Wilhelm Reich, Geza Roheim, Herbert Marcuse* (Temple Smith, 1969), p. 235.

Marxism in terms of an 'immanent critique', that is to say, it starts from the theoretical premises of Soviet Marxism, develops their ideological and sociological consequences, and reexamines the premises in the light of these consequences. The critique thus employs the conceptual instruments of its object, namely, Marxism, in order to clarify the actual function of Marxism in Soviet society and its historical direction. This approach implies a twofold assumption:

(1) That Soviet Marxism (i.e., Leninism, Stalinism, and post-Stalin trends) is not merely an ideology promulgated by the Kremlin in order to rationalize and justify its policies but expresses in various forms the realities of Soviet developments. If this is the case, then the extreme poverty and even dishonesty of Soviet theory would not vitiate the basic importance of Soviet theory but would itself provide a cue for the factors which engendered the obvious theoretical deficiencies;

(2) That identifiable objective trends and tendencies are operative in history which make up the inherent rationality of the historical process.   (p. 1)

This was a project of exceptional difficulty, and I have seen no criticism of the book written in terms of Marcuse's own statement of his 'problematic'. Once more, he worked in an area in which only specialist criticism can count, based on the same or a similar mass of textual material. In one sense the book was a success, in that it formally detached its author from the Soviet cause, but in such a way as to sustain his integrity as a Marxist. In that respect it was a buttress to a cause which grew popular in 1968, after the Czechoslovak affair; that of Marxism (or 'Marxisms') without the Kremlin.

Paul Robinson remarks in the same passage that 'One would hardly guess from reading *Soviet Marxism* that its author was simultaneously at work on an ambitious excursion into psycho-analytic theory' (p. 235). Being wise after the event, one might write that it was a book written by a man with death in his heart. Marcuse had now acceded to the Frankfurt project of matrimony between Freud and Marx; but he had characteristically given the matter his own twist. There are many Freuds, it is agreed; the one he chose was the late Freud, reacting to the same bitter events in terms of Love and Death, Eros and Thanatos. Hence the book on *Eros and Civilization*,[29] first published in 1955, which went quietly at first, but in the end made Marcuse better known and more sought after than all the rest of the Frankfurt School put together.

But perhaps it is part of the rôle of a prophet addressing such an audience: that he should be a romantic, and a puritan, and totally without a sense of humour. These two passages are my evidence from his own mouth:

I would not have mentioned Fanon and Guevara as much as a small item that I read in a report about North Vietnam and that had a tremendous effect on me, since I am an absolutely incurable and sentimental romantic. It was a very detailed report, which showed, among other things, that in the parks in Hanoi the benches are made only big enough for two and *only two* people to sit on, so that another person would not even have the technical possibility of disturbing.[30]

Spoken to an Establishment which can well afford 'obscenity', this language no longer identifies the radical, the one who does not belong. Moreover, standardized obscene language is repressive desublimation: facile (though vicarious) gratification of aggressiveness. It turns easily against sexuality itself. The verbalization of the genital and anal sphere, which has become a ritual in left-radical speech (the 'obligatory' use of 'fuck', 'shit') is a *debasement* of sexuality. If a radical says, 'Fuck Nixon', he associates the word for highest genital gratification with the highest representative of the oppressive Establishment, and 'shit' for the products of the Enemy takes over the bourgeois rejection of anal eroticism. In this (totally unconscious) debasement of sexuality, the radical seems to punish himself for his lack of power; his language is losing its political impact. And while serving as a shibboleth of identity (belonging to the radical nonconformists), this linguistic rebellion mars the *political* identity by the mere verbalization of petty bourgeois taboos.[31]

This is the fourth avatar, and the general critic faces the same difficulty. Only a specialist can challenge Marcuse on his own ground; and in this case, as in the others, he is not attacked for

29. *Eros and Civilization: A Philosophical Enquiry into Freud* (1955; Sphere Books, 1969).
30. *Five Lectures* (Beacon Press, Boston, 1970), p. 82.
31. *Counterrevolution and Revolt* (Allen Lane, 1972), pp. 80–81.

bad scholarship but for selective presentation. He has read enormously in and around Freud, and (so far as I have noted) no one attacks him for ignorance; the line of comment is that for his own purposes he has picked one aspect out of many, and in consequence presents a distorted picture of Freud. Some would even say that the Freud he chose was an old man, neurotically depressed about himself and about the world, ill-informed about politics, old-fashioned in his reading of social anthropology.

Therefore, to young Hegel and young Marx add elderly Freud, and apply the resulting compound to the politics of the 1960s. The personal commitment of an angry old man; and who is to say that in that miserable decade he was wrong to be angry?

The book on *One Dimensional Man*, published in 1964,[32] can be construed as an attempt to reach coherence and to look forward. His later work is by no means trivial, but there is a certain fluctuation of mood. At times it is that of Moses on Mount Pisgah:

And the Lord said unto him, This is the land which I sware unto Abraham, unto Isaac, and unto Jacob, saying, I will give it unto thy seed: I have caused thee to see it with thine eyes, but thou shalt not go over thither . . .
And Moses was an hundred and twenty years old when he died: his eye was not dim, nor his natural force abated.[33]

More often the mood is one of slightly theatrical despair. The critical tradition demands that its believers testify against, negate, contradict, deny any present situation which fails to reach forward towards a better future that is potentially within it. That is the duty of a critical philosopher; it is also the proper posture for a free man. Another dimension, that of criticism, must be driven at right angles through the flat plane of the present Waste Land. In this present age the resources for creating free life, for ending the repressions of civilization, are greater than they have ever been. But the affluence of these resources blunts the perceptions of ordinary men; there is not merely the repression necessary for life in society, there is surplus repression, repression not needed

32. Routledge & Kegan Paul.   33. Deuteronomy, xxxiv, 4, 7.

except to support a power structure. That power structure is all the stronger because it is unperceived, unselfconscious, pervasive; and the forces set against it are very weak. In effect, they consist of the critical philosopher, the young, the internal outcasts, the external proletariat.

The fact that they start refusing to play the game may be the fact that marks the beginning of the end of a period.
Nothing indicates that it will be a good end ... The critical theory of society possesses no concepts which could bridge the gap between the present and its future; holding no promise and showing no success, it remains negative. Thus it remains loyal to those who are without hope, have given and give their life to the Great Refusal.[34]

Alas, the scholar's peroration needs a footnote. The reference is to 'the trimmers' tortured in the outer vestibule of Dante's Inferno:[35] 'the dreary souls of those who lived without blame and without praise. They are mixed with that caitiff choir of angels, who were not rebellious, nor were faithful to God; but were for themselves ... Mercy and Justice disdain them: let us not speak of them, but look and pass.'

That is the climax Marcuse wanted; but he got it wrong. Those to whom he appeals as followers are those who *refused* to make 'the Great Refusal'. Whatever his soul's fate, it is not to live out eternity in the antechamber of Hell.

One final note. His message is that for a philosopher or a student or a black man it is better to die on one's feet than on one's knees. The doctrine is very close to that of Camus, in *L'Homme révolté* and other works, to which I return in Chapter 7; Marcuse warmly acknowledges this, and explicitly prefers Camus the mythmaker to Sartre the metaphysician.[36] Both Marcuse and Camus – surely – contributed to the mood which

34. The last page of *One Dimensional Man*, Sphere Books edition, 1968, p. 201.
35. Dante, *Inferno*, Canto 3, 11, 35–60. The translation is an anonymous one, from Dent's edition of 1900.
36. 'Sartre's Existentialism' (1948), *Studies in Critical Philosophy*, New Left Books, 1972), p. 159,

popularized the word 'identity'. But note that, on the one hand, Marcuse (till late in his career) is extremely scrupulous in using the word only in its nineteenth-century philosophic sense; he ignores the use which it has acquired in the last thirty years, not approving nor disapproving.[37] But note also, on the other hand, that the Freud whom he chooses is the late Freud, who has ceased to be a therapist seeking to heal individuals, and has sought to put the individual back into a social context. In doing so he used obsolete language about instincts and the primal horde, and Marcuse takes this over from him. But Marcuse like Freud sees identity (if I dare use the word) as both personal and social. A man (or woman) stands alone: and yet never alone. Society made him; he has no choice (if he is to be a man) but to help make society.

And it came to pass, as they still went on, and talked, that, behold, there appeared a chariot of fire, and horses of fire, and parted them both asunder; and Elijah went up by a whirlwind into heaven.

And Elisha saw it, and he cried, My father, my father! the chariot of Israel, and the horsemen thereof. And he saw him no more; and he took hold of his own clothes, and rent them in two pieces.

He took up also the mantle of Elijah that fell from him, and went back, and stood by the bank of Jordan.[38]

But there is no Elisha, nor can there be.

37. The only exception I have found is in the passage from *Counterrevolution and Revolt*, quoted on p. 69 above.
38. II Kings, ii, 11–13.

CHAPTER 7

EXISTENTIAL, ABSURD, BLACK

We have been taught to take Evil seriously.

SARTRE, *What is Literature?* (1957), as quoted by
William Barrett, *Irrational Man* (Doubleday,
New York, 1958), p. 214.

FROMM and Marcuse became 'good Americans', responding to
resonances of American feeling and cutting themselves adrift
from 'Frankfurt', Yet in a sense they remained Central
Europeans to the end. I choose that label advisedly, not
'Germans' nor 'Jews' (though they were these also), to stress
the character of that milieu and its long history of 'identity
crises' involving state and nation, religion and class.

The French case might at first seem simpler. To the identity
question, 'who am I?' surely there is a confident answer, 'je suis
français'. (Whereas you are *taught* to be an American; and in the
United Kingdom you are ridiculous if you say 'I am British', in-
comprehensible if you say 'I am English'.) To the existential
question 'am I?' there is a confident Cartesian answer, '*Cogito
ergo sum*'; of which a vulgar paraphrase might be, 'If I didn't
exist I wouldn't understand the question, would I?' A network
(rather than a dialectic) of incompatible doctrines constituted the
tradition of French thought: and in this 'the Mandarins' lived
and moved easily, with carefully regulated *angoisse*, each choosing a conceptual stance to match his location in the parallel network of French power and influence.

It does not really seem that this has been changed much by the
Fourth Republic, the Fifth Republic, the events of May 1968,
and the advent of Giscard. But no outsider can tell: and each
insider is already committed to a stance as observer and actor
within the network. I can do no more than illustrate the
character of the problem; and to do this I have chosen a triangle
of influential men, Camus, Fanon, Sartre – and what I have to

say about the third is limited, partly because the volume of his work is enormous, partly because at the age of seventy-two his views are (as always) in transition, whereas Camus and Fanon died in their prime.

The point about my triangle is that they are all influenced by existentialism; that each intersects the other two; and that each also intersects the world of politics and thought outside France.

Sartre's intellectual biography is complex; the facts of his life are simple, except in so far as he has made them intricate by his own analysis. His mother was Alsatian, a cousin of the famous Albert Schweitzer; his father (who died when Sartre was very young) was a polytechnician, and so was his stepfather; his grandfather, Charles Schweitzer, was a language scholar. It was Sartre's destiny (from the age of eight, he says) to be a professional intellectual; and he duly passed through the Lycée Henri IV to the École Normale Supérieuèr and so to the *Agrégation* (the qualifying examination for teaching at university level) in philosophy. In 1929 he took first place, Simone de Beauvoir came second; and (in some respects) they have been together ever since.

Sartre was thus committed to the profession of philosopher, and philosophy was powerful by virtue of its influence on French culture from the Sixth form onwards, though not very influential in world philosophy. Sartre was ambitious both as Frenchman and as philosopher, and at first staked his intellectual career on the tradition of existentialist thought, well established in Central Europe, not till then influential in France. Others in France followed parallel lines, but Sartre's first massive book, *L'Être et le néant*, published in 1943, won him a position as *the* existentialist; not so much because of the book, authoritative but largely unread, as because of a mood of loneliness and despair, appropriate to the last days of the Third Republic, and of a gift for presenting philosophy as myth. Few read his philosophy, a generation of intellectuals knows his novel, *La Nausée*, and (even better) his play, *Huis Clos*. Hell is an enclosed place in which three individuals torture one another throughout eternity. '*L'Enfer c'est les Autres*[1]: 'hell is other people'. Each 'identity' is alone: an identity spoiled is irretrievable. Total aloneness would be non-entity, but Sartre comes near to that pole of conceivable views. Erving Goffman (to whom the phrase 'spoiled identity' belongs) sometimes comes near to the other pole, the total immersion of the individual in others, as in a hall of mirrors. At one extreme, others are hell: alternatively, one sees oneself, one exists as ego, only through others: '*Je est un autre*'.[2]

Those who are expert can follow Sartre's intellectual history, along with that of France, through his best period as imaginative writer and myth-maker of the resistance; into the period of Cold War and revulsion against the Great Ally, Stalin; and then to the realization that Marxism need not be Stalinism, and must be redeemed from Stalinism if there were to be a future for social thought in Europe. Hence the huge work of recantation, modification, assimilation: *Critique de la Raison dialectique*, 757 pages of it, published in 1961. It is difficult to judge of the direction of influence between Sartre and his political and intellectual environment: but certainly the book (little read) stands at a key position, left of centre, a position from which two countries based on Revolution, the U.S.A. and the U.S.S.R., are both seen to be in reaction against their own traditions, and against the great European tradition. It is hard to judge just where the exact point of compromise lies between existentialism and Marxism, but certainly the work stands symbolically for 'Marxism with a human face', and this entails a move from the nihilist end of the identity scale towards concepts of the individual as conditioned by society. It could perhaps be said that Sartre leaps over the relation between individual and the small group, leaving that middle ground empty, so that the individual faces alone the historic forces of mass and class. But certainly the life of man is no longer lonely. To quote a strange phrase from Camus, at the end of a short story, it is '*solidaire*' not '*solitaire*'.[3]

For Anglophones, at least, Sartre lacks charm, and so does his

1. *Huis Clos* (Gallimard, Paris, 1947, p. 182).
2. Quoted without source, George Steiner, *After Babel* (1975), p. 26.
3. 'Jonas', *L'Exil et le Royaume* (Gallimard, Paris, 1957), p. 176.

dear friend, Simone de Beauvoir: it is easier to admire their courage, intellectual, moral and physical. 'He ventured neck or nothing' and in Browning's terms he deserves a grammarian's funeral:

> This man decided not to Live but Know –
> Bury this man *there*?
> *Here* – here's his place, where meteors shoot, clouds form,
> Lightnings are loosened,
> Stars come and go! let joy break with the storm.

Camus, from a radically different origin in society, came close to Sartre at one point, and then swung away. Perhaps when he died in a car accident in January 1960 he was swinging back towards a realignment with Sartre in face of the events of the 1960s.

He was born in a small town in Algeria in 1913; his mother was a Spanish resident, his father a French *colon* of rather low status, who was killed as a private and a conscript on the Marne in 1914. Camus and his brother were brought up in poverty by their mother; clearly he was born with outstanding gifts, intellectual and physical, but it is due to her as well as to a succession of fine teachers[4] that he did indeed find 'the career open to the talents', and was by 1939 (though he never sat the *agrégation*) a young intellectual in Algiers fully equipped to hold his own with his contemporaries in Paris.

In the 1930s he was a member of the Communist Party (Sartre never has been) but he had left it before 1939, probably over the development of Communist participation in Spain. Here, as in some other respects, one can compare him with André Malraux, whose work and creed he admired, though he never became a Gaullist.

Like Sartre, Camus ran myth and philosophy in double harness: his outstanding pre-war works, the novel *L'Étranger*

---

4. In *Le Mythe de Sisyphe* he particularly mentions Jean Grenier of the University of Algiers, and his book, *La Choix*. Grenier remained a life-long friend and wrote a valuable memoir, *Albert Camus* (*Souvenirs*), (Gallimard, Paris, 1968).

and his statement of philosophical position, *Le Mythe de Sisyphe*, got through to publication in 1942, in spite of the war, and by that time he was well recognized in Paris: recognition which was reinforced when he came forward in public at the Liberation of Paris as clandestine editor of *Combat*, then certainly the best organ of the non-Communist resistance.[5]

I am not sure if Camus alone originated 'the philosophy of the absurd': he does not in his early work acknowledge debts, as he does fully in *L'Homme révolté*,[6] published in 1951. But in its first form it is clearly a response to the politics and literature of the 1920s and 1930s; to my mind it also shows the mood and temperament of a young 'outsider' seeking to make his mark by paradox and radical logic. His object in fact is to talk down the fashionable radicalisms of existentialism and nihilism by carrying their logic to more logical conclusions – conclusions which out-flank them and roll up their battle-line from the left, to finish with victory in the centre.

As always, it is difficult for an English-speaker to come to terms with French philosophy. To begin with, *absurde* cannot be taken to mean 'absurd', unless we can strip the latter of implications such as 'ridiculous' and 'funny'. Man's condition is absurd but by no means funny, and perhaps the nearest equivalent is to take the word in the sense of *reductio ad absurdum*: rigorous deduction from the premises produce logically impossible conclusions, therefore the premises must be wrong. But Camus's premise is that 'all men must die', which cannot be denied; therefore man must live with the incongruities of his condition, as a natural being who is not part of nature. It would be incongruous to escape by suicide – into what? But given these premises how can it be logical to live?

Camus's description of the predicament is as powerful as any such statement since 'the death of God' as Nietzsche perceived it; his moral conclusions seem noble but banal. Life must be lived by reason, in terms of the Cartesian canons of lucidity and

---

5. It died at last in July 1974.
6. Paris, 1951; English translation by Anthony Bower, *The Rebel* (Hamish Hamilton, 1953; Peregrine, 1962).

clarity and *évidence* – among the moral values are *grandeur*, *honneur*, *orgueil*, *fierté*, *le désespoir qui reste lucide*[7] – and it must be lived with comrades, though it contains experiences of exile and separation, and each 'dies alone'. The myth is that of the heroes and anti-heroes of Joseph Conrad,[8] whose deaths are incongruous, whose quality is that of their persons – Nostromo, Lord Jim, Axel Heyst – not of their success or failure in action. In English terms, it is an appeal to classical education – the death of Socrates, the cry of Ajax in the Iliad, when the gods wrapped the battlefield in mist: 'Kill us, yes: but in the light of day.'

One little twist, and the heroes may seem ridiculous rather than absurd,

> Out of the night that covers me,
> Black as the Pit from pole to pole:
> I thank whatever gods may be
> For my unconquerable soul.[9]

Give it a different twist, and this is *Heroes and Hero-Worship*, in Carlyle's proto-fascist manner. Or it can seem to be (in the style of Oakeshott) an appeal to live within a heroic tradition.

But I concur with Conor Cruise O'Brien's view that Camus is better as writer than as philosopher; a master of French prose[10] and also a master of ambiguities which present a more subtle picture of moral predicaments than do the myths of Sartre.

7. The last phase is from *Le Mythe de Sisyphe; Essai sur l'Absurde* (Gallimard, Paris, 1942), p. 90.

8. The cross-reference is made by Conor Cruise O'Brien in his little book on *Camus* (Fontana, 1970), p. 84. I know of no evidence that Camus had read Conrad; but, in a Conrad manner, *The Plague* has a collective hero, the men of honour: Dr Rieux, the narrator, Tarroux, Father Paneloux, Rambert, Grand, Dr Castel, Othon, of whom only three survive.

9. The poem is in *The English Poets*, ed. T. H. Ward (Macmillan, 1919), Vol. 5, p. 504 – with other poems by W. E. Henley, some much better, some much worse.

10. 'The ideal delineation of faultless prose': *The Rebel*, p. 229. And the elegant pedantry of Clamence, early in *La Chute*: 'Ah! je vois que vous bronchez sur cet imparfait du subjonctif. J'avoue ma faiblesse pour ce mode, et pour le beau langage, en général' (*La Chute* [Gallimard, Paris, 1956], p. 10, and C. C. O'Brien, p. 76).

Leaving that aside, there are two further political points; then the question of the word *identité*.

Given his personal experience, one would expect Camus to be concerned with poverty and with colonialism. Not so: he aims straight at the excellences of the top league, the Paris circle; and for twenty years he uses Algeria simply as background for universal characters.[11] He and Fanon seem to pass one another without contact: Camus moving from Algeria to Paris, Fanon from Paris to North Africa.

The second political point is that once the Liberation honeymoon was over Camus moved away from Sartre, not to outright contradiction, yet to the opposite side of the Cold War divide. C. C. O'Brien[12] says that Camus was an unconscious collaborator in the Congress for Cultural Freedom, an American 'front' in the Cold War. So were many others, and there is not much in that. But in his second philosophical work (a learned and valuable one), *L'Homme révolté*, though his respect for Marx is still high, his denunciation of the consequences of Lenin is as shrill as any to be found in American writing of that period. Indeed the theme of the book is that revolution entails power and is doomed by logic and history to bring back the relations of master and slave;[13] and that the free man is a rebel, not a maker of revolution. Freedom is rebellion: to stand one's ground against anyone who claims to be master, and so to achieve such equality between men as is possible within man's limits.

L'Homme révolté was published in 1951. It would need very careful reading of Camus's journal articles in the 1950s to know how his mind and moods responded to the events of those years. Perhaps he would have converged again towards Sartre in face of the Algerian War, de Gaulle's restoration, the Indo–China

11. Germaine Greer, *Camus and Sartre*, 1972 (Calder & Boyars, 1974), p. 66, disputes this against Conor Cruise O'Brien and asserts that Camus broke with the Communist Party, because of its cynical attitude towards Muslim sufferings in Algeria.

12. P. 62; and see his fn. 7.

13. P. 41. 'All power tends to be unique and solitary. One must kill and kill again: the masters will destroy each other in their turn' . . . 'Prometheus ends his days as Onan.'

War and the events of 1968. Or perhaps he would have gone with Malraux, who ended a radical career as a radical Minister of Culture under his ambiguous hero, de Gaulle. All one can say with certainty is that in the short stories collected as *L'Exil et le Royaume* in 1957 Camus began for the first time to write (not very well, I fear) of *colon* and *indigène* in Algeria; and that in his last novel, *La Chute*, published in 1956, his protagonist is a man who has succeeded easily in everything, and then hears laughter, disembodied laughter, friendly laughter, laughter at his expense. And so gradually he slips away from success into dissolution; or into selflessness? Camus himself makes the old point somewhere, that an author is not to be identified with his character: and the utterances of Jean-Baptiste Clamence are in fact Delphic or Sibylline. But perhaps in his last years Camus felt himself trapped, in a personal rather than in a political sense.

I suggested earlier (p. 73) that with Sartre and Camus goes Fanon. The West Indian islands of Martinique and Guadeloupe were and still are reckoned to be parts of metropolitan France, not 'colonies'. That was also the status of Algeria, but it was eroded morally by the distinction between French citizens and those (virtually all the *indigènes*) who lived under Islamic law, not French law. There was no such distinction in the West Indian islands, themselves participants in the Revolution, and there was (or so Fanon grew up to believe) a clear distinction in everyone's mind between 'black Frenchmen' and 'negroes'. I have no information about his family, but clearly he stood high in the scale of colour, and was as brilliant as Camus in his performance within the French educational system, uniform throughout 'France'. He was born in 1924 or 1925, came to France after war service as an officer with the Free French, and went through full academic training in medicine and in psychiatry at the University of Lyon, qualifying in 1951. He was a potential leader in his profession; he was black, but also privileged.

This set up strains, and he learned the trade of writer (for which he was very gifted) in the articles on 'spoiled identity'

(Goffman's phrase) which came together in *Peau Noire, Masques Blancs*, published in 1952.[14] But the stress which broke the tenor of his career came in his professional experience as a psychiatrist treating Algerians in France,[15] and it led him first (in 1953) to a post for which he volunteered, at a psychiatric hospital at Blida in Algeria, then (in 1956) to resignation in protest against the incompatibilities entailed,[16] then to the medical service of the F.L.N. (National Liberation Front), then to editorship of their periodical in Arabic, then to a quite special position (as Algerian representative with Nkrumah in Lagos) in the politics of African liberation and unity in the years 1959, 1960, 1961. In December 1961 he died of leukemia, at the age of thirty-six or thirty-seven.

Fanon's path crossed that of Camus, and his only planned book, *Les Damnés de la Terre*, was published in 1961 with an enthusiastic preface by Sartre (a little too long, as usual). The English translation of its title, *The Wretched of the Earth*,[17] does it no justice: the book is about damnation (a word which in English now evokes a giggle), the damnation of some men by other men, and the cure for it.

The book takes a position of extreme radicalism on the colonial question. It is tagged as Marxist by the occasional use of Marxist 'fetish words', such as dialectic, contradiction, consciousness, historic mission. But Fanon was neither a Marx scholar nor a Party man, and he seems to use these words not for analysis but as insignia, or badge, or colour. The power of the book lies partly in the specific character of his clinical experience

14. Parts of this, he says, nearly became his professional dissertation. The first French edition was by Editions du Seuil; English translation by Charles Lam Markmann, Grove Press, 1967, MacGibbon & Kee, 1968, Paladin, 1970.

15. See the Chapter on 'Medicine and Colonialism' in *A Dying Colonialism* (Maspéro, Paris, 1959; English translation, Haakon Chevalier, *Monthly Review Press*, New York, 1965; Pelican, 1970) and 'The North African Syndrome' in *Toward the African Revolution* (Maspéro, Paris, 1964; English translation, Haakon Chevalier, *Monthly Review Press*, 1967).

16. His letter of resignation is at p. 62 of the latter.

17. French ed., Maspéro, Paris, 1961; English translation by Constance Farrington, MacGibbon & Kee, 1965; Penguin, 1967.

and his understanding of the techniques and ethics of his trade. He shows how there emerges a psychiatry of the colonized, rooted in the compulsions both of the masters and of the subjects, and he learns bitterly the psychiatry of guerrilla war. He is as lucid (and terrifying) about the traumata of ordinary policemen psychologically exhausted by their work as torturers as about the lasting damage to those tortured. He sees both sides clearly, though totally committed to one by a steady growth of his direct experience. Likewise, he sees both sides clearly as regards the cause of African unity and African liberation. Indeed he foresaw in the late 1950s[18] the dilemmas of Africa after decolonization; the pragmatic pressures towards the creation of a new élite of African officials, land-owners and business men, narrow in vision, no less, no more, attractive than other natural men living their selfish lives in mutuality with their dependants.[19] He rated F.L.N. 'officers' very high,[20] had no experience of other soldiers, and missed a key element in the neo-colonial situation. But if he had lived, one would have trusted his judgement on that too.

Perhaps the words 'style' and 'judgement' characterize him best. But there was also infinite devotion and hard work: and there is a direct link through psychiatry to the professional work of Erikson and other European psychiatrists in the U.S.A. To pin this down, one would have to search out Fanon's few professional articles and the references they give. It seems clear from his political writing that he was not a Freudian, but was at home with the work of Freud and his divergent successors.[21]

The point made, as briefly as possible, has been that these three Frenchmen lived political doctrines under fire, and that these doctrines are hard to specify without using (as I have done) the word 'identity'. Only Camus writes as if events had com-

18. Perhaps as early as 1957: see the references to 'neo-colonial' at p. 98 of *Toward the African Revolution*.

19. 'The Pitfalls of National Consciousness', Chapter 3 of *The Wretched of the Earth*.

20. 'This Africa to come': *Toward the African Revolution*, p. 187.

21. There is one reference to American 'psychosociology': *The Wretched of the Earth*, p. 231, fn.

pelled him, in his own person, to kill: but all three lived in the social circle of ambush, torture and violent death. So too had the Central European exiles in the U.S.A., but at one remove. The events of Central Europe were (if that is possible) even more horrifying than those of the French Resistance and the Algerian War. Yet only Walter Benjamin, of the 'Frankfurters', lingered too long, and he died by his own hand, at the crossing of the Pyrenees, in September 1940.[22]

This effect of distance might even intensify experience; no moral distinction is intended.

I should like to show that in this range of experience and philosophy there is a common element which deserves to be called a doctrine and concept of 'political identity'. I doubt whether this can be proved; but perhaps it can be 'shown'.

To take Camus first.[23]

In *Le Mythe de Sisyphe* the first person singular holds the centre of the stage. There is an astonishing piece of prose at the beginning of the chapter on *La Liberté Absurde* in which the word 'je' and its derivatives occur twenty-six times in a paragraph of twenty-five lines, and that solitary character, 'I', is the hero of both the early books, *Sisyphe* and *L'Étranger*. As C. C. O'Brien points out, this is even intensified by what he calls, 'the colonial "they", the pronoun that requires no antecedent'.[24] The Algerians 'nous regardaient en silence, mais à leur manière, ni plus ni moins que si nous étions des pierres ou des arbres morts' (p. 64). 'Je' is alienated from 'nous' – though Camus is never (in what I have read) caught in the toils of that mismanaged word, alienation.[25] In the second pair of works, *The Plague* and *The Rebel*, the emphasis on the first person singular is still there

22. See Jay (1973) p. 198, and the reference he gives to Arthur Koestler, who was a member of the same party of travellers (*The Invisible Writing* [Collins & Hamish Hamilton, 1954]).
23. The decision whether to quote in French or in English has been a matter of luck depending on availability in libraries.
24. C. C. O'Brien (1970), p. 23.
25. 'Alienating oneself from reality' appears in Bower's English translation of *The Rebel*, p. 252; the French is 'é'loigner du réel', *L'Homme révolté* (Gallimard, Paris, 1951), p. 356.

but it is differently shaped. For instance, they 'thus had realized perhaps, for the first time, the uniqueness of each man's life; now . . . they took an interest only in what interested everyone else, they only had general ideas, and even their tenderest affections now seemed abstract, items of the common stock.'[26] This is shown in action in the second speech of the proud Jesuit, Father Paneloux: 'He spoke in a gentler, more thoughtful tone than on the previous occasion, and several times was noted to be stumbling over his words. A yet more noteworthy change was that instead of saying "You" he now said "We" ' (p. 207). 'No longer were there individual destinies; only a collective destiny, made of plague and the emotions shared by all' (p. 157).

To match this, there is a philosophical recantation in *The Rebel*. The *Cogito*, previously almost solipsist in Camus, becomes 'I *rebel* – therefore we *exist*' (p. 28); and the book is largely shaped within this framework. Antiphonal to the revised *Cogito* comes this, towards the end. 'The artist, whether he likes it or not, can no longer be a solitary . . . Rebellious art also ends by revealing the "We are" and with it the way to a burning humility' (p. 240). But this is still the instantaneous 'We' of existence and rebellion. It is vain (p. 246) to replace 'we are' by 'we shall be': that would be to abandon rebellion and freedom for revolution and power.

Does Camus then go still further, totally to attenuate and disintegrate individual 'identity'? There are these passages in *The Rebel:* 'But a character implies a public; the dandy can only play a part by setting himself up in opposition. He can only be sure of his own existence by finding it in the expression of others' faces. Other people are his mirror' (p. 48). 'Man must be acknowledged by other men. All consciousness is, basically, the desire to be recognized and proclaimed as such by other consciousnesses. It is others who beget us' (p. 108). The argument could be sustained that in *La Chute*, a work of penitence, the disintegration of 'I' becomes total. 'Quand le portrait est terminé, comme ce soir, je le montre, plein de désolation: "Voilà hélas, ce que je suis." Le réquisitoire est achevé. Mais, du

26. *The Plague*, p. 171.

même coup, le portrait que je tends à mes contemporains devient un miroir.' 'Alors, insensiblement, je passe, dans mon discours, du "je" au "nous". Quand j'arrive à "voilà ce que nous sommes", le tour est joué, je peux leur dire leurs vérités (pp. 161–2).

So far as concerns Camus, I rest my case on these quotations: Camus is talking about 'identity', mine and ours. But his use of the word *identité* and its kindred is remarkably cautious. The nearest I can get to the American usage is this: 'Undoubtedly the master enjoys total freedom first as regards the slave, since the latter recognizes him totally, and then as regards the natural world, since by his work the slave transforms it into objects of enjoyment which the master consumes in a perpetual affirmation of his own identity' (*The Rebel*, pp. 109–10). Here the old senses of 'identity' are dead. But the following makes one pause:

From the moment that he strikes, the rebel cuts the world in two. He rebelled in the name of the identity of man with man and he sacrifices this identity by consecrating the difference in blood. His only existence, in the midst of suffering and oppression, was contained in this identity. The same movement, which intended to affirm it, thus brings an end to its existence. It can claim that some, or even all, are with it. But if one single human being is missing in the world of fraternity then this world is immediately depopulated. If we are not, then I am not ... (pp. 245–6)

This surely is clean prose, not burdened by decaying metaphor. He means what he says, that man is *identical* with man: humanity is *one*, and is despoiled by any exclusion, even the smallest.

The words 'slavery' and 'freedom' are continually in Camus's mouth,[27] yet he virtually ignores questions of colour and colonialism. Whereas Fanon's world is built round these concepts, and in at least one place he clashes sarcastically with Camus (not by name). 'All the Mediterranean values – the triumph of the human individual, of clarity and of beauty – become lifeless, colourless knick-knacks. All those speeches seem like collections

27. Self-parodied, in *La Chute* (p. 153). 'Vous voyez en moi, très cher, un partisan éclairé de la servitude ... Autrefois, je n'avais que la liberté à la bouche.'

of dead words; those values which seemed to uplift the soul are revealed as worthless, simply because they have nothing to do with the concrete conflict in which the people is engaged.'[28] Yet Fanon asks the same 'identity question': 'In reality, who am I ?'[29] And like Camus he moves from the question of 'I' to the question of 'We'. And one can almost watch his 'we' expanding, from Martinique, to France, to Algeria, to African unity, as the war and his personality develop. And he is bitterly familiar with 'dual identity'.

It will be also quite normal to hear certain natives declare, 'I speak as a Senegalese and as a Frenchman' . . . 'I speak as an Algerian and as a Frenchman . . .' The intellectual who is Arab and French, or Nigerian and English, when he comes up against the need to take on two nationalities, chooses, if he wants to remain true to himself, the negation of one of these determinations. But most often . . . they cannot or will not make a choice.[30]

There is an extreme statement in his letter of resignation from French government service.

Madness is one of the means man has of losing his freedom. And I can say, on the basis of what I have been able to observe from this point of vantage, that the degree of alienation of the inhabitants of this country appears to me frightening.

If psychiatry is the medical technique that aims to enable man no longer to be a stranger to his environment, I owe it to myself to affirm that the Arab, permanently an alien in his own country, lives in a state of absolute depersonalization.

What is the status of Algeria ? A systematized de-humanization.

The events in Algeria are the logical consequence of an abortive attempt to decerebralize a people.[31]

28. *The Wretched of the Earth*, p. 36. There is a sarcasm about Cartesianism on p. 241. For Camus's 'Mediterranean' myth, see *The Rebel* (p. 264): C. C. O'Brien describes this as Camus's 'most lamentable Mediterranean-solar-myth vein' (p. 56).
29. *The Wretched of the Earth*, p. 200.
30. op. cit., pp. 175–6.
31. *Towards the African Revolution*, p. 63.

Perhaps his logic moves here too readily from psychiatry to politics. But the political stance he reaches is familiar enough; human dignity, man as a being both within and outside nature, the 'right to constitute a people'.[32]

32. op. cit., p. 155.

CHAPTER 8

SPOILED IDENTITY

To prescribe activity is to prescribe a world; to dodge a
prescription can be to dodge an identity.

ERVING GOFFMAN: *Asylums: Essays on the Social
Situation of Mental Patients and Other Inmates*
(Doubleday, New York, 1961), p. 170.

IT is not easy to place Erving Goffman in the present sequence,
or indeed in the spectrum of the social sciences. He describes the
focus of his interest very modestly, as being 'to develop the study
of face-to-face interaction as a naturally bounded, analytically
coherent field – a sub-area of sociology'.[1] The next sentence
moderates even that ambition: 'To do this one must come to
terms with the fact that the central concepts in the area are ambiguous, and the bordering fields marked off badly.' Later in the
book (p. 85), he refers even more deprecatingly to 'perspectives',
of which his own is merely one.

Yet his influence reaches further than his claims, and probably
it will be found that in the long run his usage of the word
'identity' has been more influential (and more productive) than
that of Lucian Pye and the Committee on Comparative
Politics.[2]

In part his work can be defined by what he is trying *not* to do.
There is an oblique indication in a footnote to *Stigma*.[3] 'Just as
there are iatrogenic disorders caused by the work that physicians
do (which then gives them more work to do), so there are
categories of persons who are created by students of society, and
then studied by them.' So much for *The Politics of the Developing*

1. Preface (p. ix) to *Strategic Interaction* (Pennsylvania University Press,
1969).
2. In particular, the short book called *Stigma: Notes on the Management of
Spoiled Identity* (Prentice-Hall, Englewood, 1963; Penguin, 1970).
3. p. 167, fn. I.

Areas; not that he refers to the Committee on Comparative Politics, or indeed to political science at all. In so far as he has a technique (as distinct from a style), it is that of the single-handed anthropological observer, not encumbered by too much gear, too many colleagues, too heavy a conceptual apparatus. Yet though he travels light, he travels fast and far. He deprecates the massive vanities of organized social science and social philosophy, yet from his supposedly humble perspective he takes a very wide view. There is perhaps a touch of the 'pride that apes humility'; the range of his knowledge in science and literature is enormous, he is extremely sensitive to nuances of spoken and written language, and each of his seemingly simple essays has to be read for itself and also for the context which he implies.[4]

Therefore, I make no apology for using Goffman's work to close and round off this section of the book. The texture and feeling of his thought is very different from anything cited hitherto; and yet it may serve to form and exemplify the modern obsession with personal identity, social identity, and their inter-relation.

The topic or perspective is that of social interaction in small groups, generally face to face, and a key concept is that of 'face',[5] about which more below: this puts him close to various forms of transactional theory and games theory. But such theories imply an 'economic' situation, one of exchange between pre-existent individuals,[6] whereas Goffman's methodological assumption is that from his perspective it is useful to assume that the individual exists only in situations of social interaction; that it is not to say that there is no such thing as a really subsistent unique individual but that progress can be made, new things can be said, by direct and independent observation of the process of interaction.

4. It is perhaps characteristic that of the books of his that I have, none has a bibliography; only *Relations in Public: Microstudies of the Public Order* (Basic Books, New York, 1971) has an index of authors cited.

5. See the essay 'On Face-work: An Analysis of Ritual Elements in Social Interaction' (1955), republished in *Where the Action Is*.

6. For instance, in G. C. Homans, *Social Behaviour: Its Elementary Forms* (Routledge & Kegan Paul, 1961).

The closest analogies are those of linguistics and ethology. The study of language is clearly a study of interaction; there is a philosophical problem concerning the conceptual possibility of a solipsistic or private language, but if a private language existed it could not be studied empirically in an inter-personal way. The beginning of meta-language, of theory about language, is to draw back from talk, to put oneself outside it and to listen analytically. Similarly, in the last thirty years, ethology or social biology has transformed natural history by making the assumption that a possible perspective or universe of discourse is that of animals in interaction with one another. This is now so familiar that there is no need to multiply examples of territoriality, aggression, nuptial ritual, mutual recognition: concepts now refined and made technical, which were at first used in a rather anthropo-morphic way. Indeed one model for Goffman's method is that of social anthropology as a discipline of field study; and there was certainly something in common between the development of his work in the 1950s and that of the quite independent Manchester group, led by Gluckman and Devons at the same period, who thought in terms of introducing the methods of social anthro-pology into the study of Western industrial and social institu-tions.[7] There is however a gulf fixed, in that the Manchester group were concerned with structure and function in a society as a whole, and in the dynamics of change; whereas Goffman is by implication critical of the 'macro-study' of structure and function, though he admits them in the analysis of face-to-face interaction.

Goffman's major pieces of field-work in depth were concerned with one of the Shetland Isles,[8] in the early 1950s, and with a large public mental hospital in the U.S.A. Among his other sources have been direct observation of the human species in 'gatherings' and 'encounters' of all kinds; wide reading of

7. For instance, in the work of Tom Lupton, Bill Watson, Ronnie Frankenberg.
8. Work for a Chicago Ph.D., based on Edinburgh University: much quoted but still not formally published. He was born in Alberta in 1922 and took his B.A. at Toronto.

novelists (the late Ivy Compton-Burnett, for instance) whose
story structure and style of dialogue depend on small but intricate
patterns of social interaction; and books of etiquette, ancient and
modern, which (used in this way) prove to be based on astute
observation of the proprieties of social intercourse and the
penalties entailed by infringement.

Add to this his wide reading, the individual flavour of his prose
style, his gift for illuminating quotation, and one can safely recom-
mend Goffman (in moderation) to the intelligent amateur in
sociology.[9] There are now eight books and collections of
articles, as well as the unpublished thesis. There is perhaps 'a
school', in the sense that Goffman had much influence on
Garfinkel and ethnomethodology, till recently fashionable. But
the essence of Goffman's work evades dogmatism and it falls
dead once it is stripped to the level of a text-book.

It may be best to approach his work on 'spoiled identity'
through his essay 'On Face-work'.[10] The plain English word
'face' has convenient ambiguities. A 'face' (taken as referring to
body-image as a whole) conveys the individuality of a person;
not only his features, but the voice, the mannerisms, the walk –
and (for dogs, and even for blunt human senses) the smell. But
there is also a common usage of 'putting the best face on it', and
the related remark 'I must put my face on', which implies that
the speaker is either woman[11] or actor. The image of performance of a rôle before an audience is of great importance to
Goffman as an analytic tool – 'The world's a stage and all the
men and women merely players.' Finally, there is the phrase
fashionable at the moment – 'I got egg on my face over that, I
fear': and so to the Victorian translation of some unknown
Chinese word as 'face'. This last and most general concept of
'face' refers to rituals of behaviour which are functionally
necessary to the avoidance of social friction; Goffman always
thinks first of interplay between intellectuals of Anglo–

9. But don't start to dream of Goffmanese, as I did while working on this
Chapter.
10. Above p. 8–2 fn. 5.
11. Goffman often quotes Simone de Beauvoir.

American society, but he generalizes quite effectively to 'Shetland Isle', to 'Central Hospital',[12] to China and other traditional societies. The basic rule is never to lose face. Therefore, never act so as to cause another to lose face. Therefore, if another is acting to save your face, be tactful about his attempt at tact, even if he bungles it; and so on, the social incident fading to infinity down the hall of mirrors.[13] The delicacy of mutual interaction is very great, even in quite rough societies. Such delicacy varies greatly as between individuals, but from this 'perspective' (Goffman's word), this is to be regarded as skill rather than as virtue. As strongly as anyone (once he has taken his white coat off) he likes some people and detests others, prefers pride, honour and dignity to their opposites. But when he is playing the role of objectivity, he *sees* himself as playing the role of objectivity, and he knows the rules and risks of 'stepping out of role'.

And so to *Stigma: Notes on the Management of Spoiled Identity*. It seems clear that Goffman came to this first because of his work in *Asylums*. It was not in his style to write a book like that of Thomas Szasz on *The Myth of Mental Illness*;[14] indeed he makes no claim to speak as psychotherapist.[15] But as a sociologist professionally skilled in observation it is his business to be delicately aware of the pattern of social interactions in a mental hospital, in terms of rôles, fronts, faces, functionally necessary pretences. All but the most deeply regressed patients (and even some of these) are participants in social interaction and aware of their own performance. I have no idea what in-

12. Both fully explained in *Behavior in Public Places*, p. 4.

13. 'The infinite regress of mutual consideration that' (G. H. Mead's) 'social psychology tells us how to begin but not how to terminate' (*Stigma* p. 30).

14. (Paladin, 1972). See also Goffman's references to articles by Szasz, in *Asylums: Essays on the Social Situations of Mental Patients and Other Inmates* (Doubleday, New York, 1961; Pelican Books, 1968), p. 297 fn. of Pelican edition.

15. Though he is sometimes unkind to them: for instance, *The Presentation of Self in Everyday Life* (Doubleday, New York, 1959), pp. 132, 154; Pelican Books, 1971; and often in *Asylums*.

fluence he has had on psychiatry, if any: but there is much in common with the stress on social factors in psychiatry, now popularly known through Bettelheim, Szasz, Laing, Cooper, Esterson, and others. Thus the 'crucial case' of spoiled identity is that of the former inmate of a mental hospital. He (or she) knows something about himself which is known to some interlocutors and not to others. The pattern of interaction will vary accordingly, from risk of embarrassment when talk gets near certain topics, to risk of loss of job and livelihood. The 'stigma' must be 'managed'; and (to anticipate the conclusion of the argument) there are in any society many forms of stigma; there is much to be learned about the interaction of the stigmatized and the 'clean': but in the last resort none of us is without stigma,[16] and we must respect our own risks and those of others. Again, interaction is a hall of mirrors. '*Nous sommes tous coupables.*'[17] '*Mutato nomine de te Fabula narratur.*'[18] ' – *Hypocrite lecteur – mon semblable – mon frère.*'[19]

And so to definitions: and it should perhaps be said that Goffman's style in definition is part of his method. The definitions are not very precise, linguistically or operationally. Neither would be relevant, because he does not propose to attempt either deductive argument or measurement. They are a plain guide to the reader about the use of certain common words in 'Goffmanese': and (as in a natural language) understanding is deepened by experience of the use of each word in a 'Goffman' context. It is therefore desirable to proceed so far as possible by direct quotation.[20]

When a stranger comes into our presence, then, first appearances are likely to enable us to anticipate his category and attributes, his 'social identity' – to use a term that is better than 'social status'

16. *Stigma*, pp. 152, 153.
17. A recurrent theme in Camus's *La Chute* (e.g. pp. 127, 134, 151, 153).
18. Horace, *Satires*, I, i, 69.
19. Baudelaire, Preface to *Les Fleurs du Mal*.
20. The quotations which follow are from *Stigma* (Chapter 1, 'Stigma and Social Identity'), pp. 12–14.

because personal attributes such as 'honesty' are involved, as well as structural ones, like 'occupation'.

We lean on these anticipations that we have, transforming them into normative expectations, into righteously presented demands.

... the demands we make might better be called demands made 'in effect', and the character we impute to the individual might better be seen as an imputation made in potential retrospect – a characterization 'in effect', a *virtual social identity*. The category and attributes he could in fact be proved to possess will be called his *actual social identity*.

The term stigma, then, will be used to refer to an attribute that is deeply discrediting, but it should be seen that a language of relationships, not attributes, is really needed. An attribute that stigmatizes one type of possessor can confirm the usualness of another, and therefore is neither creditable nor discreditable as a thing in itself. For example, some jobs in America cause holders without the expected college education to conceal this fact; other jobs, however, can lead the few of their holders who have a higher education to keep this a secret, lest they be marked as failures and outsiders.   (pp. 12–13)

There are three 'grossly different' types of stigma:

First, there are abominations of the body – the various physical deformities. Next there are blemishes of individual character perceived as weak will, domineering or unnatural passions, treacherous and rigid beliefs, and dishonesty, these being inferred from a known record of, for example, mental disorder, imprisonment, addiction, alcoholism, homosexuality, unemployment, suicidal attempts, and radical political behaviour. Finally there are the tribal stigmata of race, nation, and religion, these being stigmata that can be transmitted through lineages and equally contaminate all members of a family.   (p. 14)

Can any reader of Goffman or of this book claim to be exempt from all such blemishes?

But the stigmatized identity will not be (or will only rarely be) without support from 'sympathetic others'. There are three categories. First, those who share his stigma. Goffman has studied in some detail the emergence and the *mores* of formal organizations created to speak for those crippled physically in various ways. But remember that there are also 'the tribal stigmata of race, nation and religion' (p. 14): once outside the society of those who bear our stigma each of us is stigmatized. Then (secondly) there are the 'wise': 'wise' neither in the sense of the wisdom of Solomon nor in that of 'wise guy', but in that of 'wise to . . .'

Wise persons are the marginal men before whom the individual with a fault need feel no shame nor exert self-control, knowing that in spite of his failing he will be seen as an ordinary other.
Before taking the standpoint of those with a particular stigma, the normal person who is becoming wise may first have to pass through a heart-changing personal experience, of which there are many literary records. And after the sympathetic normal makes himself available to the stigmatized, he often must wait their validation of him as a courtesy member. The self must not only be offered, it must be accepted.   (p. 4)

Thirdly (to some extent included in the second category) there are those on whom the stigma (as it were) rubs off: the convict's child, the alcoholic's wife, the mother of a mental defective, and so on.
All this is concerned with social identity. I think that for Goffman this is the same as role identity: but he may well have changed his mind about it. His early work adopts a 'dramaturgi-cal' perspective,[21] but there is an essay first published in 1961,[22] which states classically the entanglements in which sociologists may be involved if they use the role concept carelessly.
Social identity is to be distinguished from personal identity: and that in turn from ego identity. The last of these was the main concern of Erikson, the Frankfurt 'critics' and the French metaphysicians.

21. *The Presentation of Self in Everyday Life* (1959).
22. 'Role Distance', in *Encounters; Studies in the Sociology of Interaction* (Bobbs-Merrill, Indianapolis, 1961).

Both types of identity can be better understood by bracketing them together and contrasting them to what Erikson and others have called 'ego' or 'felt' identity, namely, the subjective sense of his own situation and his own continuity and character that an individual comes to obtain as a result of his various social experiences.

Social and personal identity are part, first of all, of other persons' concerns and definitions regarding the individual whose identity is in question.

On the other hand, ego identity is first of all a subjective, reflexive matter that necessarily must be felt by the individual whose identity is at issue. Thus, when a criminal uses an alias he is detaching himself from his personal identity; when he retains the original initials or some other aspect of his original name, he is at the same time indulging a sense of his ego identity. Of course, the individual constructs his image of himself out of the same materials from which others first construct a social and personal identification of him, but he exercises important liberties in regard to what he fashions.

(*Stigma*, p. 129)

Social identity and ego identity are difficult to sort out: the concept of personal identity is relatively simple, indeed it harks back to the old bureaucratic notion of identity as record or dossier, a 'biography' (Garfinkel's word, writes Goffman, p. 81) which exists interpersonally and is 'on the record', so that it goes on when the person as 'ego' exists no longer. The concept generates in a quite straightforward way a chapter about 'Information Control and Personal Identity' (Chapter 2 of *Stigma*): straightforward at least in principle, but of course subject to problems of secrecy, mystification, misunderstanding and mutual tact about the questions: 'Who knows what about whom from what sources?' and 'Who tells what about whom in what contexts?'

Ego identity is much more relevant to the present topic and much harder. One reason may be that Goffman has never been happy about the status of reports on introspection as evidence for anything beyond themselves, nor about discussion of moral issues from the standpoint of moralist.

First, he writes of professional advice about how to accept and live with stigma, but under this heading creep in references to

Sartre's book on *Anti-Semite and Jew*[23] and to the literature of 'authenticity', thus ambiguously commended:

> It should be noted that although the literature on authenticity is concerned with how the individual ought to behave, and is therefore moralistic, nonetheless it is presented in the guise of dispassionate neutral analysis, since authenticity is supposed to imply a realistic reality-orientation; and in fact at this time this literature is the best source of neutral analysis concerning these identity issues.
>
> (p. 135 fn. 16)

But the in-group thus defined has no existence except in 'a language of relationships' (*Stigma*, p. 13): it has meaning only in relation to a recognized out-group, the group which stigmatizes:[24]

> The in-group and the out-group, then, both present an ego identity for the stigmatized individual, the first largely in political phrasings, the second in psychiatric ones. The individual is told that if he adopts the right line (which line depending on who is talking), he will have come to terms with himself and be a whole man; he will be an adult with dignity and self-respect.
>
> And in truth he will have accepted a self for himself; but this self is, as it necessarily must be, a resident alien, a voice of the group that speaks for and through him.

> You cannot be honest with yourself until you find out what you are and, perhaps, consider what society thinks you are or should be.
>
> (p. 149)

Thus, even while the stigmatized individual is told that he is a human being like everyone else, he is being told that it would be unwise to 'pass' or let down 'his' group. In brief, he is told he is like anyone else and that he isn't – although there is little agreement among spokesmen as to how much of each he should claim to be. This contradiction, this joke is his fate and his destiny. It constantly challenges

23. Grove Press, New York, 1960. Goffman refers to Sartre also in *Relations in Public: Microstudies of the Public Order* (Basic Books, New York, 1971), p. 248.
24. This is the point of H. G. Wells's powerful myth, 'The Country of the Blind' (1904) (reprinted in *Selected Short Stories*, Penguin, 1958).

those who represent the stigmatized, urging these professionals to present a coherent politics of identity, allowing them to be quick to see the 'inauthentic' aspects of other recommended programmes but slow indeed to see that there may be no 'authentic' solution at all.

(p. 150)

Goffman would (I am sure) hate to have imposed on him the concept of dialectic: in this hasty reading of all his work I have not found it once, not even to express antipathy.[25] But here (one might say) is not dialectic but dilemma: it is part of Goffman's method to leave it hanging unresolved.

The fourth chapter (or 'essay') in *Stigma* is called 'The Self and Its Other'. 'The role of normal and the role of stigmatized are parts of the same complex, cut from the same standard cloth' (p. 155). 'The stigmatized and the normal are parts of each other: if one can prove vulnerable, it must be expected that the other can, too' (p. 161). It can be shown by observation (p. 159) that 'two-headed role-playing', a switch of roles, 'for fun or seriously' is by no means uncommon. Can one then regard this situation as one that can be universalized, at least potentially? Can we take it that stigma involves 'a two-way social process in which every individual participates in both roles, at least in some connections and in some phases of life' (p. 163)? Can one 'I' have several 'we's? The answer clearly is 'Yes': a conclusion still enigmatic.

25. He excludes less firmly an existential language: note his references to authenticity (p. 135 and p. 150), and this from the essay on 'The Self and its Other' – 'The norms dealt with in this essay concern identity or being, and are therefore of a special kind.'

Part Three
APPROPRIATE USE

And the Gileadites took the passages of the Jordan before the Ephraimites: and it was so, that when those Ephraimites which were escaped said, Let me go over; that the men of Gilead said unto him, Art thou an Ephraimite? If he said, Nay;
Then said they now unto him, Say now Shibboleth; and he said Sibboleth; for he could not frame to pronounce it right. Then they took him, and slew him at the passages of Jordan: and there fell at that time of the Ephraimites forty and two thousand.

Judges xii, 5-6.

Each tongue hoards the resources of consciousness, the world pictures of the clan. Using a simile still deeply entrenched in the language awareness of Chinese, a language builds a wall around the 'middle kingdom' of the group's identity.

GEORGE STEINER, *After Babel* (Oxford University Press, 1975) p. 232.

In Sir Thomas Browne's magnificent phrase, the speech of a community is for its members 'a hieroglyphical and shadowed lesson of the whole world.'

ibid., p. 465.

CHAPTER 9

TACTICS

'THE temptation . . . to use [those] words which are most likely to attract attention and excite belief in the importance of [one's] subject is almost irresistible.'[1] 'Sartre has said, in speaking of the term 'existentialist': 'The word is now so loosely applied to so many things that it no longer means anything at all.'[2] 'Using the term "alienation" without explaining any further what one has in mind communicates little more today than does tapping one's glass with one's spoon at a banquet: neither does much more than attract attention.' 'It has become a fetish word, and people seem to delight in finding ever different uses of it.'[3]

All these quotations have been lifted from the last chapter of Richard Schacht's important book on *Alienation* (1971), and I think they can be transferred bodily to a discussion about identity. Indeed the words alienation and identity often work in double harness, as symbols which together express everything and nothing about personal and social anguish in the last third of the twentieth century. I had not discovered Schacht's book when I first lighted on this subject, but we seem to have passed through similar phases of thought at much the same time: admiration of a word, study of it in detail, scepticism, disillusion, an attempt to reach a new realism.

The first part of this book records a search conducted in three phases. First, an observation of the spreading use of the word 'identity' in the daily and weekly press. Its use grows so wide (spreading even to the sports columns) that all meaning is eroded; the word falls within the terms of the quotation from Ogden and

1. C. K. Ogden and I. A. Richards, *The Meaning of Meaning*, 1923 (Routledge & Kegan Paul, 1966).
2. Sartre, '*Existentialism is a Humanism*', in W. Kaufmann (ed.), *Existentialism from Dostoevsky to Sartre* (Meridian, New York, 1956).
3. pp. 237–8.

Richards,[4] in that writers use it not to convey meaning but as a badge to mark their style of writing and their cultural aspirations. It is (to be frank) generally a mark of bad style and silly aspirations.

But the second stage of search, that into the history of the word, and its passage through different languages and contexts, is much more interesting. Chapter 2 does something to sketch the wanderings of a word through the history of more than two thousand years. Since Aristotle's time the word has found a place for itself in philosophy, theology, mathematics, individual psychology, group psychology, the organization of bureaucratic society. It is a 'rich' word, in that it has many contexts, most of them important. It is not surprising that it has recently been used to confer status rather than to convey meaning.

The third phase of search reinforces this sense of ambiguity and of 'riches' or 'bigness' or 'scope'. Perhaps ambiguity is one of the ways in which a word grows big. And eventually it grows so big that it is empty. But I hope the pursuit of identity through a linked series of contemporary writers has shown that there is still something there. Some of them (Pye, Erikson, Fromm, Goffman) seek to give the word a technical sense, loosely defined and not the same in each case. Marcuse, Sartre, Camus, Fanon do not use the word much, and certainly do not treat it technically in the context of social identity. Yet surely they are talking about the same 'thing' as the other four? Behind the word lie a common problematic, a common concept? It would be a victory if one could ensnare the concept, settle an appropriate use of the word.

But certain lines of approach are blind alleys, at least for the present writer.

Firstly, this is not a book about philosophy or linguistics or the debatable ground which they hold in common and contest. I

4. Or of this. 'I think the learned word' [in this case the word 'supernatural'], 'on the strength of a very superficial relation of meaning to the thing the plain man had in mind, was simply snatched at and pummelled into the required semantic shape, like an old hat. Just so the people have snatched at once learned words like *sadist*, *inferiority-complex*, *romantic*, or *exotic*, and forced them into the meanings they chose.' C. S. Lewis, *Studies in Words* (Cambridge University Press, 1967), p. 67.

could claim the late J. L. Austin and the late T. D. Weldon as friends, so that I know how the argument goes. But I cannot resolve it, and perhaps no one can. I refer to Austin's work below, but only in respect of his remarkable ear for subtleties of usage. In the debated area of words, concepts and things I must proceed cautiously but amateurishly, without seeking precision.

Secondly, I am more professionally concerned with what might be called the 'I/we' problem in general. But that also overlaps and links different disciplines. I come to it from the side of political study; but one soon becomes aware that it is a problem also for other empirical disciplines, such as linguistics, various branches of psychology, sociology, social and cultural anthropology, perhaps even economics (although the last named tries to evade the problem by the device of 'methodological individualism').[5] I am convinced that it is right in principle to sustain and develop the unity of the social sciences, but I am equally convinced that one cannot talk about everything at once. I began with 'political identity', and intend to treat that as unifying concept for this book. But it cannot be discussed except within a wider context, and therefore I must in the next chapter attempt to delimit 'political', at least for the purpose of the present argument.

Thirdly, my purpose is primarily empirical. That is to say, I am looking for a framework of exposition that will do the primary scientific job of accommodating observed facts.[6] Of course in

5. See for instance S. Lukes, 'Methodological Individualism Reconsidered', in A. Ryan (ed.), *The Philosophy of Social Explanation* (Oxford University Press, 1973), and my *Power, Violence, Decision* (Peregrine, 1975), p. 202.

6. This is my attempt to translate the old Greek maxim σώξειν τα φαινό-μευα, literally to 'save appearances', as in Milton's marvellous lines about God and the astronomers:

(*Paradise Lost*, viii, line 9)

'Hereafter, when they come to model Heaven
And calculate the stars, how they will wield
The mighty frame, how build, unbuild, contrive
To save appearances, how gird the sphere
With centric and eccentric scribbled o'er,
Cycle and epicycle, orb in orb'.

'saving appearances' thus, one also to some extent defines what observations are to be taken as relevant, and thus builds conclusions into one's premises. But this happens in any practical enquiry, however rudimentary, and it works, in the sense that it serves to gain a handhold on the 'phenomena', and a tentative lead towards manipulation, and even prediction. A Ptolemaic astronomy, as Milton points out, may be so far wrong that even Jehovah is moved to laughter; but it served its turn.

Fourthly, this book, though empirically oriented, is also of necessity conceptual. In the next chapters I am more concerned to construct an argument, and to maintain the links in it, than to offer empirical conclusions or to persuade the reader by an extensive use of examples. At each stage of the argument examples can be found, and indeed there have been relevant scholarly investigations using many different techniques. But my object is not to present a summary of these, but to 'ensnare the concept' by shaping a construct of links and sequences.

After the next chapter, which deals with the definition of politics, the sequence is as follows.

Chapter 11 chooses a starting point: the linguistic character of first person singular and first person plural. This is an attempt to illustrate the character of the problem in the broadest and most familiar terms. But this cannot be regarded as a logical foundation for what follows: partly because what is familiar is also complex, partly because I have not found any good studies of the inter-relation between language, social behaviour and the perception of self, directed specifically to this topic. At best, I hope to show what kind of problem this is, and why I approach the problem of political identity through the problem of political language.

The second state (Chapter 12) is concerned with another broad generality – that 'I' is linked to 'We' by the process of 'identification with . . .' I have chosen what may seem a trivial example, that of *Dreams about H.M. the Queen* because this may come home to the reader more effectively than would a report on the scientific literature of psychotherapy. I could not in any case have made a complete survey: for what my opinion is worth, I feel that the mass of case material encompassed by the concept is overwhelming and yet the nature of the process is unclear. In Chapter 13 the argument becomes specifically political, in terms of shared interest and shared territory, the strengths and weaknesses of these concepts or forces. Chapter 14 deals quite briefly with the famous abstractions, the historical rhetoric of political identity, in terms of nation, race, religion, class. In the present period each of these is under pressure, in a practical sense and also in an intellectual sense. They are going the way of the city – state and its gods, the medieval church, the feudal kingships and their 'ceremony'.[7] The phrase or concept 'political identity' will not be of much use to us unless we can give it a deeper and more permanent foundation, which will 'accommodate' these 'phenomena' and also others, which exist now and are likely to persist.

In Chapter 15 I attempt to close the arch by adding, as coping-stone or key, the concept of language 'in an extended sense'. This will include not only the nuances of vocabulary and accent, their continuing shifts of pattern, but also the linked concepts of myth, ritual, symbolism and ideology. These are not unfamiliar to the social sciences; but general theory is still weak and political scientists (with a few distinguished exceptions) have done little to develop the study and use of concepts which are absolutely essential to the understanding of the play of political action, at any level, high or low.

7.   'And what have kings, that privates have not too,
                    Save ceremony, – save general ceremony ?
                    And what art thou, thou idol ceremony ?'

        Shakespeare, *Henry V*, IV, i, line 242.

CHAPTER 10

THE DEFINITION OF 'POLITICAL'

IT is better to do one's subject than to define it. To adapt a remark attributed to Bernard Shaw, those who can do the subject show what it is by doing it; others are involved in disputes over definitions.

But some attempt must be made here because the argument started quite informally from usage of phrases such as 'political identity', or 'the crisis of identity in new states'. Six of the eight authors referred to in detail are deeply involved in politics; the two exceptions are Erikson and Goffman, whose specific concerns are with 'ego identity' and 'social identity'. But I hope I have made it clear that these forms of analysis, political, individual, and social, cannot satisfactorily be disentangled; indeed, the theory (in so far as there is anything that can be called a theory) is about their mutual entanglement and inter-play.

Nevertheless, the scope of investigation must be narrowed in order to bring it into focus; this is a book about politics. One way to proceed is by stipulative definition, and it would not be difficult to parade twenty or thirty definitions of 'politics', 'the study of politics', 'political science', which have been tried out in the course of academic demarcation disputes. But the process is distasteful, and in any case it is ineffective. The last thirty years has been a stimulating period in political science precisely because so many intruders have broken into the traditional territory;[1] a short list would certainly include social psychology, sociology, cultural and social anthropology, administration and management, and economics. It would be pointless, indeed crippling, to erect a barrier to exclude them.

But there are two familiar expedients which can be used to evade the problems of stipulative definition. One of them is to look at current usage in regard to the word 'politics' and its

1. Hence my earlier book, *Politics and Social Science* (Penguin, 1967).

kindred, some of them rather ugly: 'political', 'politicking' (from the notional verb 'to politick'), 'politicize', 'politician' and a few more (the worst so far is 'depoliticization'). In fact, the words are used differently by different people in different sub-cultures: and the key word shifts its sense slightly in different languages – *politique*, *politik*, *politico*, and even between English usage and American usage, between neo-Marxist usage and neo-liberal usage. Any generalization about usage would be hard to test.

I suggest however that there is a central core of meaning, and a metaphor.

The former is concerned with questions of power and authority, with contests to secure them, and with their exercise within a recognized framework of government. That will not do as a stipulative definition, because one is involved in circular argument as soon as one begins to make the terms more precise. The phrase 'power-and-authority' is itself a battlefield of disputation; in English it is really more like a synonym for politics than an explanation, and one cannot be at all sure that there are French, German, Italian, Russian words which can simply be put in the place of the English words. Indeed, one of the older traditions of analysis is to see what happens when one makes play with the corresponding family of words in Latin and Greek. Similarly, it is not easy to say what 'a recognized framework of government' is, without being pushed back into a circular reference to 'the supreme political authority', whether it be city, or state, or feudal empire.

Nevertheless, we can say with some confidence that in ordinary usage the word 'politics' is primarily concerned with such things as parliaments, presidents, parties, public officials, cities and city bosses, enforcement of law, civil liberties, dictatorships – and so on. It is concerned with 'them', the powers, the big boys, the fixers, the 'high heid yins'; not in general but as a special trend or sector of our grumbles about the human situation. That is where 'politics' bites first and most deeply.

But then the reflective person and the wit find analogies to that process everywhere; there is the politics of the shop floor, of the football league, of the local amateur dramatic society, of the university (the *Microcosm*, as in Francis Cornford's little book),[2] and (quite relevantly and consistently) *The Politics of the Family*.[3] The list can be extended indefinitely, and one may well ask whether the metaphor is still alive or whether it is passing over into a new usage of the word 'politics', more general than the old one. Personally, I think that the metaphor still has life. Cornford's phrase 'Young Academic Politician', still has a sharp edge to it, at least in the context of his sections on 'parties', 'caucuses', 'on acquiring influence', 'the political motive', 'prevarication', 'squaring' – and so on. When Ronald Laing coined the title, *The Politics of the Family*, for a book about Schizophrenia, he probably knew nothing of political science, still less of Cornford; nevertheless, the metaphor indicates the new slant that he proposes to give to his material.

In fact, the metaphor is sufficiently alive to provoke discussion, to ask for generalization, at whatever level of sophistication is appropriate to those participating. It sets going the idea that perhaps politics is not simply about 'them' but is an aspect of all human interaction, something implicit in the social character of man.

But ordinary usage, I think, is still primarily concerned with the politics of the Polis, or of whatever is to be regarded as its contemporary equivalent.

The second expedient is that of recourse to authorities. Who wrote books about politics which are respected even when disclaimed? What sort of things did they write about? There is no canonical list; and the names that occur to one are by no means easy to sort out into categories such as philosophers, improvers, empirical social scientists, historians. The list includes, for instance, Plato and Aristotle, who find it essential to discuss politics as one aspect of the nature of man and of good or bad living: Thucydides, who wrote what Cornford characterized as mytho-

2. *Microcomographia Academica, being a guide for the Young Academic Politician* (Bowes, 1908, 8th ed., 1970); or in Lord Snow's *The Masters* (1951).
3. R. D. Laing (Tavistock, 1971).

logical history, [4] the narrative of a tragedy in Greek politics; St
Augustine, his mind set on the City of God, St Thomas Aquinas,
writing in the tradition of Aristotle; the paragons of standard
examination papers, Hobbes, Locke, Rousseau; the uncertain
path of empirical investigation and advice, which perhaps begins
in the modern world with Machiavelli and Harrington, ends for
the present with the last Ph.D. thesis recognized as fit for a
degree in 'politics'. The older books are part of the substance of
our culture; and they give us leave to take a very broad view of
'politics', if that takes our fancy. But they also set quite precise
and exalted standards for the conduct of argument about
politics, including argument about the observation of politics.

The best formula I can find is that of 'common purpose'. That
is to say, the 'great books' are about communality, about social
entities, but only to the extent that they are or may be capable of
purposive collective action.

'Action' or 'act' is a word that belongs to the individual person, who decides for or against action. 'Purpose' also is a word
correlated with individual reason; a man chooses purposes,
reasons about means to end, reviews his purposes in the light of
reasoning about means and of experience of success or failure.

Yet common purpose is not a combination of words that makes
nonsense. It comes easily off the tongue, or off the typewriter;
and we can pile up examples of strong or weak common purpose,
of common purpose imposed by a single man, as by Hitler in the
German people, of the breakdown of common purpose.

A discussion of *political* identity is perhaps primarily a discussion of the conditions in which it is possible to realize 'common
purpose'.

But Jean Blondel in a recent book refers rightly to 'the vast,
windy temple of political thinking'.[5] The reader should at least
be aware that contrary winds blow through this transparently
simple phrase. For Oakeshott[6] there are two modes of conduct,

4. *Thucydides Mythistoricus* (Arnold, 1907; reissued by Routledge & Kegan
Paul, 1965).
5. *Thinking Politically* (Wildwood House, 1976), p. 25.
6. *On Human Conduct* (Clarendon Press, 1975).

which must not be confused, that of living together and that of
acting together; there is a clear cut between 'civility', the
political order under law, and 'an enterprise association', the
administered implementation of a pre-determined purpose. The
modes may coexist, but must not be confused. Whereas Blondel,
as I understand him, takes a unitary view of politics, as a process
of decision-making about collective goods.

There is perhaps not so much between us as may seem at first
right; draughty the temple is, but we are all in it.

SHARED IDENTITY

The employment of language to sanctify action is
exactly what makes politics different from other
methods of allocating values. Through language a
group can not only achieve an immediate result but also
win the acquiescence of those whose lasting support is
needed. More than that, it is the talk and the response
to it that measures political potency, not the amount
of force that is exerted. Force signals weakness in
politics, as rape does in sex. Talk, on the other hand,
involves a competitive exchange of symbols, referential
and evocative, through which values are shared and
assigned and coexistence attained. It is fair enough to
complain that the politician is not deft in his talk, but
to complain that he talks is to miss the point.

MURRAY EDELMAN, *The Symbolic Uses of
Politics*, Illinois University Press, 1967, p. 114.

THE most familiar and therefore least noticed kind of identity is
grammatical; expressed by the personal pronouns, in particular
'I' and 'we', and also by inflexions, in these languages which
have inflected verbs. Greek and Latin, for instance, can be
relatively sparing (compared with English) in the use of the
nominative of personal pronouns, and in consequence these often
come with special emphasis.

Surely there must be a discussion of this topic somewhere in
the vast literature of comparative linguistics. There is, for instance, a very interesting analysis[1] of the use of second person
singular and second person plural, in those languages in which
the distinction between Thou and You, both treated as singular,
still marks a strong social distinction, as in French and German.

1. R. Brown and A. Gilman, 'The Pronouns of Power and Solidarity'
(1960) in P. Giglioli, ed., *Language and Social Context* (Penguin, 1972); see
also Chapter 5, p. 105 ff., of Peter Trudgill, *Sociolinguistics: An Introduction*
(Penguin, 1974).

Hence the important French verb '*tutoyer*', and the social analysis which it implies. To whom and in what contexts is it appropriate to use '*tu*' rather than '*vous*'? In marginal cases what is the tactical implication of bending the conversation towards '*tu*' or towards '*vous*'? There are complications because in some languages (for instance, Italian and Spanish) there is a third possibility, that of the honorific third person singular *lei* or *usted*, shortened forms of *la vostra Signoria* and *vuestra Merced*. And there are various periphrases such as the use of 'one' or '*on*', or of the passive, or of impersonal verbs (as in Latin and Greek) which postpone or dodge the choice between more or less honorific ways of addressing 'the significant other'.

G. H. Mead[2] bases much of his analysis on the antithesis of 'I' and 'we'; Martin Buber's[3] prose poem *Ich und Du* (I and Thou – or should it be I and You?) has been immensely influential; George Steiner's, *After Babel* (p. 97) has a brief excursion on I/thou/he; Sartre in *L'Être et le Néant* has a chapter on ' "L'Être avec" (Mitsein) et le "Nous".'[4] And there is this by George Macdonald Fraser in a review of a book about Field Marshal Slim (Fraser is the creator of 'Flashman', and a good judge of military *nuances*).[5] At the end of the war, speaking of the Japanese army, he told a Burma reunion; 'You tore it apart.' How many generals would have resisted the temptation to say 'we'? It wouldn't even occur to Slim.[6] Yet I have no bibliography for 'I/We', and my analysis is in that sense naïve.

The first point to make is that, although I and We occur in all Western languages, there seems to be no logical necessity about this, in that 'one' can (if 'one' has to) find periphrases by which to dodge them. I have allowed the word 'I' to appear fairly freely

2. *Mind, Self and Society: from the standpoint of a social behaviorist* (Charles W. Morris ed., Chicago University Press, 1934).

3. 1923; translated and edited by Walter Kaufmann, (T. & T. Clark, Edinburgh, 1970); V. W. Turner (1974, pp. 47, 68, 251), refers to Buber's essential We: I doubt if this is relevant here.

4. *Essai d'ontologie phénoménologique* (Gallimard, 1943), pp. 484–503. The chapter includes a quite baffling discussion of the French word '*on*'.

5. Ronald Lewin, *Slim: The Standardbearer* (Leo Cooper, 1976).

6. *Glasgow Herald*, 2 December 1976.

in this text: but it would not be difficult to edit it out by writing 'the present writer' or by using the passive or various impersonal forms. In English it perhaps seems slightly odd to dodge the first person singular persistently. But there are some cases (a leading article, for instance, or a scientific paper) in which it is clearly wrong to use the words 'I' or 'me'; wrong because there are contexts in which impersonality is necessary and appropriate. And there are curious cases when one refers to oneself in the third person; the case of a child using his or her own Christian name because his or her grasp of the pronouns is not very strong; the sophisticated case in which the speaker pretends to stand outside his own skin and to contemplate *Ego* ironically; the case of stiff formality – 'For the Duchess, An invitation from the Queen to play croquet'; 'From the Queen, An invitation for the Duchess to play croquet'.[7]

Similarly in the first person plural. To say 'we' is to imply propositions about sharing one's being with others, and one may well be shy about making such a commitment. Indeed, 'we' is sometimes a rhetorical device, a matter of manipulation, venturing delicately to put people together in a bundle which includes oneself. And these difficulties can almost always be mitigated by periphrases.

It is said that this is characteristic of linguistic usage in Japanese; and one can see how it might be possible to construct a language without 'I/We' and the corresponding verbal forms.[8] But I cannot imagine a social entity that lacked such meanings as 'I-ness' and 'we-ness', extravagant concepts, and very hard to manage philosophically, even when disguised as ego-identity and social identity.

One component in the history of the word 'identity' is the notion of an entity that persists, that is the same through time. It is quite appropriate that the Open University should take this theme as a basis for one of its introductory courses in philosophy,[9]

7. *Alice in Wonderland*, Chapter 6.
8. After writing this, I came on a science fiction book which postulates just such a society: Robert Silverberg, *A Time of Changes* (Gollancz, 1973). The mythological task of the hero is to change this.
9. Gordon Vesey (ed.), *Personal Identity* (Open University Press, 1973).

since it can serve as a type case of a problem that is essentially philosophical. As soon as we reflect on the conditions of there being any discourse at all, we light on the puzzle of 'things' that 'persist' through 'time'. It is a matter of common sense, observation and generalization that no *thing* persists through *time*. Time is flow; the succinct Greek of Heraclitus pinned this down in two words some time in the fifth century B.C., and Lucretius more pragmatically said the same in Latin hexameters in his poem about *The Nature of Things*, a title taken over by an Oxford philosopher in the 1970s.[10] No material object endures without change; yet the persistence of objects is a condition of discourse. What then endures? And so to philosophizing about the persistence of non-material 'things', a theme which has itself 'persisted' from Plato to the present day.

Approached in this way, the 'identity of a person' is only one case of a general philosophical problem, that of persisting things, and so far as I could trace it in Chapter 2 the personal use of the word 'identity' appeared fairly late in its history. But there is nothing reprehensible about that use of language, nor in its extension to the use of the first person plural as long as we do not let it confuse us. For instance, each and every human being has a physiological identity; there is something in each body which permits physiologically and 'rejects' the grafting of 'alien' tissues. But that is not the same sort of 'identity' as that of the self-conscious observer, 'I': grammatically, 'we' is cast for a rôle analogous to that of 'I' and the analogy is sometimes overpowering.

If you have young children, you can observe quite early that with language they acquire the possessive adjective of the word 'I': 'mine' is spoken (at least in our family experience) almost as soon as the word 'no', and both of them are markers of a phase in the development of self-assertion.

My personal impression is that 'I' and 'mine' appear before 'we' and 'ours', which are concepts adding another dimension of difficulty, that of shared identity.

10. A. M. Quinton (Routledge & Kegan Paul, 1973).

Perhaps there are some children who never learn the 'proper' use of the word 'we'; they acquire its usage by imitation, but have no sense of its binding force, its emotional colour. Be that as it may, there seems now to be a consensus among professional students, in many related disciplines, that the development of language is not conceivable except in relation to 'significant others'. A 'Kaspar Hauser'[11] baby, reared in silence and isolation like a Kaspar Hauser bird, has no language – has no means of saying 'I'. Yet the potentiality of speech is inborn, as is illustrated by the very difficult and delicate process of training a child born blind and deaf.

What is mine I appropriate: what is ours we share. What is mine is not yours: 'we' exclude 'them' from what 'we' share. Are there human 'instincts', is it part of the physiological inheritance of man to appropriate to himself and also to share with others ? There one merely staggers from one difficult question to another. Recent work on animal 'ethology' has put together a store of observed facts which were at first generalized in terms such as 'territory', 'personal space', 'aggression', 'bonding', 'ritual', which interpret animal behaviour through human analogies. It is clearly illegitimate to play these analogies back, and to 'prove' that in these respects men share a biological inheritance with other social animals. The second generation of ethologists are well aware of this, and are trying to purge their scientific language of anthropomorphic implications. It is very interesting to watch and understand birds and animals; but one has to hold firmly to the fact that none of them, not the most expressive of birds or apes, has any notion of saying 'I' or 'we' or 'they'.[12] They can smell it, perhaps, and act it out, but they cannot say it. I do not think that it helps us with the present problem, which is profoundly concerned with language (with 'How to Talk', in

11. A film was made recently about his story; *The Enigma of Kaspar Hauser*, by Werner Herzog, the West German director.

12. But see Eugene Linden, *Apes, Men and Language* (1975; Penguin, 1976). Chimpanzees are not physiologically equipped to speak, 'but can they learn and use sign language designed by themselves ?' The question remains open.

J. L. Austin's phrase[13]), if we push the inquiry back to the physiological inheritance of behaviour.

Can one read more than 'appropriation', 'sharing', 'exclusion' into the apparent simplicity of the personal pronouns? Quite small children can be fiercely possessive about items of 'property'; must it then be argued that 'private property' is 'natural'? Certainly not, unless equal standing is conceded to 'common property', 'ours', which has an equally good basis both in language and in anthropological observation. There are rather more interesting questions about sharing in material and in non-material 'things'. Perhaps the latter, such things as language, accent, rituals, religious beliefs, ways of livelihood attract the word 'ours' more readily than the word 'mine': the 'folk ways' (to use W. G. Sumner's word)[14] are in their nature things held in common. But it is quite usual to find individuals as much attached to 'my way of doing things' as to 'my tools', the physical objects which become expressions of something abstract. It is not altogether easy to distinguish concrete and abstract in the speech of ordinary people.

Another problem arises because, at least in complex societies, the use of 'we' depends on context; 'we' the family, 'we' the local community, 'we' the craftsmen, the teachers, the medical profession, and so on. One 'I' can have many 'we's'; but perhaps 'I' also is to some extent context-dependent. There may or not be a unique and persistent identity resident somewhere in each of us: but certainly our individuality shifts a little according to context, chooses different words and gestures, gives priority to different interests, according to the 'we' which temporarily has the upper hand in the social context. 'I' is certainly not fixed and eternal, 'we' subsidiary and fleeting.

Thence one passes to the difficult questions of objective and subjective sharing, of unconscious and self-conscious solidarity. One of the strongest linguistic indicators is given by the con-

13. 'How to Talk: some simple ways' (1952), J. L. Austin, in *Philosophical Papers*, J. O. Urmson and G. J. Warnock (eds.), (Clarendon Press, 1961), p. 181.
14. *Folkways: a study of the sociological importance of usages, manners, customs, mores and morals* (1907; new edition Dover, New York, 1959).

texts in which appear the words 'I', 'we', 'they' and their correlates; yet if we examine ourselves introspectively we cannot define very readily what these contexts are. One has to listen to oneself (as it were) and to note one's own use of the word 'we'. There is a practical sense in which one uses it explicitly but 'unconsciously' in different circumstances as they arise; and there is a practical difference between that situation and one in which one chooses deliberately to say 'we', whether one does so astutely, as a rhetorical device, or ethically, as a public statement of one's commitment.

The problem concerns particularly class and nationality, which provoke the metaphor of 'waking' into a new consciousness, and thus gaining new strength.

It is possible to define 'working-class' statistically by various indicators; it is not very easy to establish a satisfactory set of operational definitions, but even when that has been done, with the highest available expertise, the result is merely a *category*. The proletariat is not in the Marxist sense a *class*, a participant in history, unless it has class consciousness and the resulting solidarity.

It is not self-evident that selfconsciousness adds strength or effectiveness; there is certainly some truth in the old saying that in politics he travels furthest who does not know where he is going. But it is at least clear that selfconsciousness about common identity involves some structuring of the situation; the emergence of leaders to 'tell one who one is', the use of a rhetoric of identity which strengthens in each of us one 'we' against its competitors. Of course, if the leaders are foolish we travel nowhere; but without this kind of leadership and its language, it is scarcely possible to find 'common purpose' in a collectivity. There may be very rapid, but unselfconscious, social change; but that is not a political revolution.

NOTE

To round this out with examples, we would have to look first at empirical studies of speech-learning in very young children. There is nothing that I can find in Piaget, nothing in the index and bibliography of Ruth Wylie's comprehensive book on *The Self-Concept*;[15] the quite extensive literature of 'political socialization' takes up the tale too late in childhood. There is also a great range of anthropological literature, on themes which could be labelled '*We, the Tikopia*', after Raymond Firth's early book.[16] On the whole, fruitful cases are generated more freely by cultural anthropology than by social anthropology, because of its traditional connection with linguistic exploration in the styles of Sapir and of Whorf. Comparable fields in the modern world are to be found in the utterances of head teachers struggling with problems of morale in schools; and in the rhetoric of sport. The best article about the manipulation of identity that I have seen is by Don Revie, manager of Leeds United and England.

And here are two more, both from writers who have been Party members. Jean-Baptiste Clamence, in Camus's *La Chute*, describing his rhetoric of universal guilt: 'Alors, insensiblement, je passe dans mon discours, du "je" au "nous".'[17] And in Arthur Koestler's *Darkness at Noon*, the fall of the revolutionary leader Rubashov begins when 'he utters a "grammatical fiction";' he distinguishes between 'I' and 'we', between himself and the Party.[18]

There are important insights into the formation of group identities (the emergence of one 'we' and of many 'we's') in Davidson Ketchum's book about a civilian internment camp in the First World War,[19] but I have not tried to follow up that lead into the very large literature of prisoners and concentration camps.

15. *A Critical Survey of Pertinent Research Literature* (Nebraska University Press, 1961).
16. *A sociological study of Kinship in primitive Polynesia* (1936; 2nd ed., Allen & Unwin, 1957).
17. *La Chute*, p. 162.
18. Arthur Koestler, *Darkness at Noon* (Jonathan Cape, 1941; Penguin Books, 1964): I owe this reference to H. M. Drucker, *The Political Uses of Ideology* (Macmillan, for the London School of Economics, 1974), p. 87.
19 J. Davidson Ketchum, *Ruhleben, a prison camp society* (Toronto University Press and Oxford University Press, 1965).

CHAPTER 12

IDENTIFICATION WITH . . .

Only as . . . conjoined with our affections, which com-
mix, coincide, and as it were identifi with that
grandest and Divinest Mysterie of Love, sciz. God
made Flesh.

E. HOOKER, 1683 (Quoted in N.E.D., under
'identify').

My argument about I/We might be upset, or at least extended,
if there had been a thorough exploration by a comparative philol-
ogist. Even so, I should remain convinced that one must begin
the study of political identity by cultivating an ear sensitive to
language.

There is a second matter of a very general kind. Apparently,
it was Freud, in the early 1920s, who introduced into psychoanalysis the concept of 'identification with'.[1] This is a very
powerful concept, in the sense that we feel we know what it
means. There is a clear image, almost a visual and auditory one,
of the child who 'identifies with' father, or mother, or elder
sibling; grows up through identification with other heroes; and
settles finally for identification with his own identity. Some (like
Walter Mitty in Thurber's story) are facile identifiers (Danny
Kaye acted this out for us in the film) all their lives; and are
rather nice people, even successful ones – it is not self-evident
that it is necessary for the good life that one should acquire an
identity during adolescence and stay with it until the age of
senility.

Similarly with political identification. We can readily imagine
what it would mean to 'identify with' Hitler or some other great
and terrible or lovable exemplar. But for the present purpose it
may serve equally well, or even better, to take a silly and simple
example. There is a little book called *Dreams about H.M. the*

1. Above, p. 37 fn. 5.

Queen,[2] which Brian Masters introduces thus. He revealed at a dinner party that he had an occasional dream about the Queen: 'To my amazement everyone else at the table had dreamed about the Royal Family as well'. So he began to collect examples, in a non-scientific way, and the book is the result. It is at once funny-haha, funny-peculiar and funny-serious; a most curious example of a political community in which a binding factor is that many partake in one. But the one is a mere image, a cardboard cut-out, not a person. In fact many of the dreams are about meeting the Queen and other Royalties as if they were 'real' people: the 'dream-work' gets going to domesticate the remote and to mix it with the familiar. Among the curiosities that result there is one chapter headed 'Mixed Identity' (p. 102) which deals with the case in which you not only *meet*, you actually *are* the Queen or one of her kin. These cases are introduced by this quotation from Blake:

> I dreamt a dream! What can it mean?
> And that I was a maiden Queen,
> Guarded by an angel mild:[3]

'What can it mean?' Masters illustrates various pretentious interpretations, from Aristotle's time and before it. 'Jung' (for instance) 'would recognize the Queen as an *archetype*, deeply embedded in the *collective unconscious* of the English people, a symbol which we inherit from our forebears. . . . The Queen is the ultimate hero. She is Venus, she is Ulysses, she is Robin Hood, Beau Brummel, Davy Crockett.' And so on, leading up to a Jungian analogy with the archetypes embedded 'in the ancient Tarot cards' (p. 137). Masters is witty at the expense of other dream analysts also, and passes the matter off lightly. 'The dream is not about the Queen; it is about you' (p. 139). And he quotes Hazlitt (p. 138), 'We are not hypocrites in our sleep, in sleep we reveal the secret to ourselves.'

Masters may be drawing his examples only from a particular

2. Brian Masters, *Dreams about H.M. the Queen and other members of the Royal Family* (Mayflower, 1973).
3. 'The Angel', *Songs of Experience*.

sector of society; and he is quite ostentatiously unscientific. But this (like 'I/We') is an experiment that each of us can try in a crude way. If not, with the Royal family, then with whom? This kind of quasi-empirical evidence is strengthened by what looks like the self-evidence of Euclid. Things equal to the same thing are equal to one another. Persons who identify with the same person identify with one another: they share an identity. This is in effect what Freud said (*Works*, Vol. 15, p. 121, as quoted by Erikson): 'Many equals who can identify themselves with one another, and a single person superior to them all – that is the situation we find realized in groups which are capable of subsisting.'

This seems to be (as it were) the evidence of one's own eyes, and it would be foolish to try to demolish it. But it must in fairness be reported that scholars have not been very successful in taking the matter further.

On the one hand, as Erikson says, the concept of psychosocial identification presents 'even more elusive characteristics' (than that of personal identity), 'at once subjective and objective, individual and social'. Lazowich adds more plainly that there is 'lack of agreement in describing what is meant by the term'.[4]

The stereotype is that of identification with father or mother. This is extended by analogy to identification with other 'parent figures': so loosely defined that 'that grandest and Divinest Mysterie of Love' would certainly be included. But we also get (Erikson, *Encyclopaedia of Social Sciences*, p. 63), identification with things even more abstract: 'an era's identity crisis', 'to identify with a life-style of invention and production'.

On the other hand, identification can be down-graded till it is no more than imitation (Lazowich, p. 175) – not that the imitation is altogether easy to specify. And one of the oldest examples is that of the *New Oxford Dictionary*'s quotation from Burke:

An enlightened self-interest, which . . . they tell us, will identify with an interest more enlarged and public.[5]

4. L. M. Lazowich, 'On the nature of identification', *Journal of Abnormal Social Psychology*, 51 (1955), p. 176.

5. *Reflections on the Revolution in France*, 1790.

This looks as if it were a very practical kind of identification, in the spirit of Adam Smith. But Adam Smith also said that '. . . people of the same trade seldom meet together, even for merriment and diversion, but the conversation ends in a conspiracy against the public, or in some contrivance to raise prices.'[6]

And what in any case *is* 'identification' if it is more than 'imitation' and different from it? In Freud it passes over from process to state: 'At the point where the super-ego takes the place of the parental function (introjection), identification is said to have occurred.'[7]

Indeed, careful observers (Lazowich for instance, and Ruth Wylie) are embarrassed in that 'descriptions also have been entirely qualitative in nature' (Lazowich, p. 75). Ruth Wylie says (p. 123), 'As the reader will soon realize, this particular area of research is at best an extremely confusing one.' A whole generation of students of voting behaviour have relied on the distinction between objective and subjective class: to what class does the researcher allocate the respondent, to what class does the respondent allocate himself/herself? And the distinction works, in that objective and subjective correlate differently with observed behaviour. There seems to be a factor there most easily described as 'self-identification', which has predictive force in voting studies. But (to quote Lazowich again) ' "what?" and "how?" '

These two difficulties, specification and quantification, do not mean that we have reached a dead end. The point rather is that we are involved in research, which is in Ruth Wylie's terminology 'phenomenological'; that is to say, research in which our data depend on the conscious and deliberate reactions of a respondent to stimuli; these stimuli will generally (however ingenious we may be) be in the form of written or spoken language. Psychologists are well aware of the difficulties involved, and respond to them in various ways; at one extreme by rejecting all evidence of

6. *The Wealth of Nations*, Book I, Chapter X, Part II.
7. *New Introductory Lectures*, quoted by Lazowich.

this kind, at the other extreme (and perhaps Timothy Leary[8] was an example) by escaping from attempts at measurement into attempts at what might be called trans-sensory or super-sensory communication; that is to say, transcendental identification.

The effect of these difficulties in 'cashing' what seems to be so obvious as 'identification with' is to strengthen my belief that language is the best clue; and also to give a warning that if common experience cannot be 'cashed' by definition and measurement, then we hang perilously on the verge of 'parapsychology'. It is not very difficult to find examples of identification which look like extra-sensory perception.

8. See the references to his work on measurement in the index to Ruth Wylie's book; and what he wrote after his conversion to the use of mind-bending drugs: *The Politics of Ecstasy* (1966) and *Jail Notes* (1970). 'Tune in, turn on and drop out.'

CHAPTER 13

PRACTICAL IDENTITIES

THIS chapter deals with what at first seem to be objective criteria of identities. This from Burke, quoted in the previous chapter:

> An enlightened self-interest, which . . . they tell us, will identify with an interest more enlarged and public.

And this from A. H. Clough:

> Juxtaposition, *in fine*; and what is juxtaposition? . . . Allah is great, no doubt, and
> Juxtaposition his prophet[1]

In other words, shared interests and shared space, the criteria of cooperation between practical men.

1. SHARED INTERESTS

The proposition is that those who share an interest share an identity; the interest of each requires the collaboration of all.

It does not require that there be a complete coincidence of individual interests. The closer the coincidence the stronger the bond of interest, but the theory allows for the fact that in a plural society a person may have conflicting interests, may be a member of many distinguishable 'we's'. It is then for the individual to choose between the strength of his own interests, and he will have to reckon that some interests can throw sanctions into the scales. If a man thinks of betraying a conspiratorial organization or of running away from a national army in time of war, the risk of death for desertion reinforces his shared interest in the success of the cause. Interests involve not only the pursuit of gain but the avoidance of loss, and interests may be served by violence or

1. *Amours de Voyage*, VI.

compulsion at lower levels than the power of life and death. Interests by their nature are in conflict; there may be (in a Hobbesian sense) a higher common interest in checking the escalation of conflict into mutual destruction. It is scarcely possible to discuss plurality of interests without being involved in the long debate over sovereign power and its legitimation. In the present context one can only mark that 'Serbonian bog' (Milton's simile for the debate on pre-destination) and pass on.

Similarly with the problem of kinship and common interest. We have inherited the idiom – 'blood brotherhood', 'blood is thicker than water' and so on – and it is not in doubt that kinship stated in cultural terms is a powerful factor in political and social identity. This is not simply a matter of social anthropology, nor of the power of kinship in international finance and trade, in the hands of Jews, Pakistanis, Chinese and others. One could perceive the 'cousinhood of Dukes' as a factor in English politics up to the fall of Harold Macmillan in October 1963: the common interest of the Kennedy family in American politics still persists.

But these are ties of culture, of symbolic not biological blood (adoption or marriage may impose membership on those not born with 'blue blood'). It is biologically true that the individual as phenotype is an expression of the genotype or gene-pool which existed before him (or her) and will exist after him, in a form perhaps modified by his success or failure in reproduction. It is also true that in a sense all life on earth is a 'single homeostatic system; linked by interdependence and in some respects unique and individual; and that each living individual is also unique in its capacity to discriminate and reject alien tissue'.[2] It is (in the third place) a commonplace that man achieved unique success biologically by an extreme development of the device of culture, found in other animals only in a very rudimentary form. All men share biologically in a capacity for culture and the transmission of culture; and the variety of cultures, great though it is, is in some respects limited by biological factors, the facts of birth,

2. J. Z. Young, *An Introduction to the Study of Man* (Clarendon Press, 1971), p. 114.

growth, death and reproduction. In that sense, 'the brotherhood of man' is something a little stronger than a metaphor, and so is 'man's kinship with nature'. But the arguments that arise are too complex to be handled here,[3] and I must simply as referee blow a whistle and exclude biological argument from the present field of play.

Even within that bounded realm there is an extreme disparity of views about what constitutes a common interest. At one extreme stands the view that something 'exists' which transcends individual preference and decision. It is perhaps fair to exemplify this by a quotation from the late A. F. Bentley's sparkling book on *The Process of Government*:[4]

The term 'group' will be used throughout this work in a technical sense. It means a certain portion of the men of a society, taken, however, not as a physical mass cut off from other masses of men, but as a mass activity, which does not preclude the men who participate in it from participating likewise in many other group activities. It is always so many men with all their human quality. It is always so many men, acting, or tending toward action – that is, in various stages of action. Group and group activity are equivalent terms with just a little difference of emphasis, useful only for clearness of expression in different contexts.

It is now necessary to take another step in the analysis of the group. There is no group without its interest. An interest, as the term will be used in this work, is the equivalent of a group. We may speak also of an interest group or of a group interest, again merely for the sake of clearness in expression. The group and the interest are not separate. There exists only the one thing, that is, so many men bound together in or along the path of a certain activity. Sometimes we may be em-

3. See for instance the peroration of J. Z. Young's book, p. 631; and note three recent books: E. S. Dunn, Jr., *Economic & Social Development: A Process of Social Learning* (Johns Hopkins University Press, 1971); John Passmore, *Man's Responsibility for Nature: Ecological Problems & Western Traditions* (Duckworth, 1974) and A. L. Somit (ed.) *Biology & Politics* (Mouton, The Hague & Paris, 1976), particularly the essay by Peter Corning.

4. 1908: reissued, Harvard University Press, 1967; pp. 211-12. In this mood Bentley gets close to Kurt Lewin's 'field theory' of social interaction. Cf. the references to Lewin in V. W. Turner, *The Forest of Symbols* (Cornell University Press, 1967).

phasizing the interest phase, sometimes the group phase, but if ever we push them too far apart we soon land in the barren wilderness. There may be a beyond-scientific question as to whether the interest is responsible for the existence of the group, or the group responsible for the existence of the interest. I do not know or care. What we actually find in this world, what we can observe and study, is interested men, nothing more and nothing less. That is our raw material and it is our business to keep our eyes fastened to it.

The word interest in social studies is often limited to the economic interest. There is no justification whatever for such a limitation. I am restoring it to its broader meaning coextensive with all groups whatsoever that participate in the social process. I am at the same time giving it definite, specific content wherever it is used. I shall have nothing to say about 'political interest' as such, but very much about the multiform interests that work through the political process.

I think this quotation is fair to Bentley's theory of interests, in that this is a passage in which he tries to be as concrete as he can in specifying men, groups and interests, and to 'cash' his claim that he can establish the existence of social realities which are not 'spooks' nor ideologies (see Chapter 15, below). It is also 'fair', in that Bentley consciously tries to avoid the aura of metaphysics which surrounds the basic collective entities found in Rousseau, Hegel, and Marx.

At the other extreme stands the view, not limited to economists, that 'interest' and 'individual' are the terms that belong together, not 'interest' and 'group'; and that interests can be combined only in a market (as economists would say), or 'transactionally' (the sociological term). (This is part of the definition of an interest; do not ask at this point how one defines 'exchange'). There are many variants of the view, too complex to be called a school;[5] and it is a little arbitrary to counterpoise Mancur Olson to Bentley. But it is relevant to do so, because they converge on the same point: in Olson's title, *The Logic of Collective Action: Public Goods and the Theory of Groups.*[6]

Olson begins by quoting statements to illustrate what he calls

5. See the comment by Stephen Lukes, 'Methodological Individualism Reconsidered', referred to above, p. 103, fn. 5.
6. Harvard University Press, 1965.

'The Traditional Theory of Groups'. This, for instance, by an authoritative sociologist of the last generation, R. M. McIver; 'Persons . . . have common interests in the degree to which they participate in a cause . . . which indivisibly embraces them all.'[7] Olson goes on:

> It is of the essence of an organization that it provides an inseparable, generalized benefit. It follows that the provision of public or collective goods is the fundamental function of organizations generally. A state is first of all an organization that provides public goods for its members, the citizens; and other types of organizations similarly provide collective goods for their members.   (p. 15)

But, (he continues [p. 21]):

> Though all of the members of the group therefore have a common interest in obtaining this collective benefit, they have no common interest in paying the cost of providing that collective good. Each would prefer that the others pay the entire cost, and ordinarily would get any benefit provided whether he had borne part of the cost or not.

And further: 'What a group does will depend on what the individuals in that group do, and what the individuals do depends on the relative advantage to them of alternative courses of action' (p. 23). Therefore, it is not rational to join an organization unless it is one which gives you as individual a gain bigger than your contribution and not obtainable without your contribution. This is a rather rare case. The common one is (for instance) that of O.P.E.C.; the price of oil can only rise as far as the market will allow, and the market is in the last resort governed by the paying capacity of each consumer in relation to his priorities. Why join O.P.E.C. if it imposes costs on you and gives no benefits that you would not obtain without joining? In that particular case, the costs of joining are small, and perhaps the U.K. will join when it becomes a net oil exporter if other exporters allow it. But this would not be 'rational' except on the basis of a calculation which includes other advantages. Be a 'free rider' if you can.

In fact, it is misleading to introduce the U.K. here as if it were

7. From his article on 'Interests' in the 1931 *Encyclopaedia of the Social Sciences*, VII, 147, Chapter 9, p. 3.

a rational actor. Olson's argument requires that *individuals* 'should generally be rational, in the sense that their objectives, whether selfish or unselfish, should be pursued by means that are efficient and effective for achieving these objectives' (p. 65). Trade union members rarely attend branch meetings, and yet agree that meetings ought to be attended. 'In fact the workers were not inconsistent: *their actions and attitudes were a model of rationality when they wished that everyone would attend meetings and failed to attend themselves*' (p. 86, Olson's emphasis).

So much for Olson's attack on the Western pluralist conception of group politics. The Marxist concept of a class fares no better at his hands. 'Much of the evidence suggests that Marx was offering a theory based on rational, utilitarian individual behaviour' (p. 109). But Marx is quoted as writing: 'In so far as the identity of their interests does not produce a community, national association and political organizations – they do not constitute a class.'[8] If that is the alternative he chooses, then he has introduced into the dialectic 'a metaphysical concept' ('an element of mysticism') 'which has no part whatever to play in an empirical discipline like economics' (p. 109, fn. 30). 'A worker who thought he would benefit from a "proletarian" government would not find it rational to risk his life and resources to start a revolution against the bourgeois government' (p. 106); 'Where nonrational or irrational behavior is the basis of a lobby, it would perhaps be better to turn to psychology or social psychology than to economics for a relevant theory' (p. 161).

These brief summaries are less than fair to Bentley and to Olson, and to the cohorts ranged metaphysically in either camp. But they are perhaps enough to show that the concept of 'shared interests' (though powerful) is not easy to handle. To some extent the argument is definitional; but there is also an underlying difference of opinion, not easy to specify, about what it is to be a man in society. But neither line of analysis helps much to cut through the rhetoric of shared interests and to settle

8. Olson, p. 107: the quotation is from *The Eighteenth Brumaire*, via R. Dahrendorf, *Class and Class Conflict in Industrial Society* (Stanford University Press, 1959), p. 13.

argument about specific cases. Both suffer from the same limitation: that one cannot look into a man's mind or into a group mind. The relative priorities of a man or a group are known only in retrospect, by what the economists call 'revealed preference'. What they did (and this includes what they said) alone offers a clue as to what they 'really' wanted. Diagnosis of shared interest comes after the event, not before it.

2. SHARED SPACE

Those who share a place share an identity. Prima facie this is a fair statement, whether 'the place' is taken to be 'space-ship earth'; or a beloved land; or a desolate slum or public housing scheme. Indeed, it is (like the concept of 'shared interests') rhetorically powerful because it appeals to solid sense, and it should not be allowed to melt away under analysis.

The first step in analysis is to get rid of the notion of 'natural frontiers'. No frontiers are 'natural' in the sense that they exist apart from human activity. Even to determine approximately the frontier of an ecological environment or an animal territory we must know what activity we seek to determine spatially. Human space is coterminous with human activity; to put it differently, the texture of human interaction is thicker, more dense in some patches than in others, the blank spaces on the map set bounds to those spaces where the lines and symbols cluster strongly.

Human activities are very varied and not all clustered in the same patterns. Mapping of 'journeys' has been used a good deal in attempting to determine appropriate boundaries for the administration of human communities. I am thinking in particular of the work done by W. I. Carruthers for the Herbert Commission on Local Government in Greater London, of which I was a member in the early 1960s.[9] But such research has accompanied most efforts at local government reform in recent years, and it is still in progress in relation to the 'social engineering' question, of

9. Cmd 1164, 1960.

how to define viable communities within sprawling urban areas. Research rarely produces unambiguous results even in areas (such as the Western Isles of Scotland) where the results seem to be dictated by 'the hand of nature'. The sea, the land, the air remain the same; and yet they are not the same as they were for prehistoric man working up from the South in the wake of the retreating glaciers, for Scandinavians from the North converging with Irish from the West, for reconstruction and depopulation after the defeat of the clans. *The Cheviot, the Stag and the Black Black Oil*[10] – the pattern of journeys is now changing yet again. The journeys vary according to functions (trade, job, education, health, entertainment, professional organization and so on) which affect different members of the 'community' differently; and it is not as easy as administrative planners would wish to settle a hierarchy of place corresponding to hierarchy of function.

Indeed, it soon becomes necessary to take the logical step made by Karl Deutsch in his book, *Nationalism and Social Communication*, published in 1953.[11] A journey is for a meeting ('Trip no further, pretty sweeting, Journeys end in lovers' meeting, Every wise man's son doth know'). But (except for lovers) meeting is now possible without journeys; the concept must be generalized under the rubric of social communication, which includes person-to-person contact by letter and telephone, the linking of specialists by special media, the linking of communities in a selective way by mass media. The problem is complicated further by the case of differential attention: the listener hears physically in the same way the message settling a bargain, the message reaffirming love, the weather news, the outbreak of nuclear war, the background tapestry of pop. In a sense he hears all and understands all; but not all in the same sense, and the degree of salience has so far eluded measurement except in bounded laboratory stituations, because the focus of attention shifts quickly according to context, and the acceptability of talk depends not only on a common language but on

10. John McGrath's satirical review, written for the 7/84 Company.
11. Sub-titled, *An Enquiry into the Foundations of Nationality* (Wiley and M.I.T., New York).

subtle nuances of speech and accent which provoke reactions relevant to the problem of we and they.

All these things define the social space of people interacting in networks of communication, and it is illuminating to work on the hunch that those who share a network share an identity. Even though (as in Northern Ireland) they communicate mainly to express mutual hostility, yet they are under the net, all others are 'outside'.

CHAPTER 14

POWERFUL ABSTRACTIONS
Nation, race, religion, class

IT may be useful to begin with a classical quotation from John
Stuart Mill:

A portion of mankind may be said to constitute a Nationality, if they
are united among themselves by common sympathies, which do not
exist between them and any others – which make them co-operate with
each other more willingly than with other people, desire to be under
the same government, and desire that it should be government by
themselves or a portion of themselves, exclusively. This feeling of
nationality may have been generated by various causes. Sometimes
it is the effect of identity of race and descent. Community of language, and community of religion, greatly contribute to it. Geographical limits are one of its causes. But the strongest of all is identity of
political antecedents; the possession of a national history, and con-
sequent community of recollections; collective pride and humiliation,
pleasure and regret, connected with the same incidents in the past.
None of these circumstances however are either indispensable or
necessarily sufficient by themselves.[1]

This introduces three of the recognized dimensions of political
identity, nation, race and religion, and it excludes class, the
Marxist option. The passage is written within the Victorian
framework of ideas, in the violent youth of European nationalism.
A nation is not merely a state of fact; it is a state of feeling, a
source of obligation. It demands loyalty within; externally it
demands recognition by its peers, conferred through the juridical
recognition of statehood. Some later authors attack the moral
status of nation, for instance, Elie Kedourie,[2] who sees here only
intellectual confusion and a serious danger to the peace and
stability which most men want – or at least ought to want. But

1. *Representative Government* (1861), Chapter XVI, 'On Nationality, as
connected with Representative Government'.
2. *Nationalism* (Hutchinson, 1960, 3rd edition, 1966).

very little has been added[3] to Mill's definition, which emphasizes the reinforcement of the unstable concept of 'nation' by the equally vague concepts of 'race' and 'religion'. But there is no end to debate about the conflict or convergence of the concepts of 'nation' and of 'class'. Does, or should, nation override class, or class nation?

One can simplify a little by setting out recent views of race and religion as elements of identity.

RACE

The word 'race' is now virtually discredited, along with the German *Rasse* and *Volk*, after a long and confusing period of popularity. There are two very ancient factors. One of them is the notion that kinship creates a special tie. On the one hand, this is reinforced by physical metaphors and proverbs: shared blood, shared semen ('the loins of David'),[4] 'blood brotherhood', 'blood is thicker than water'. On the other hand, there is world-wide evidence of the creation of kinship by fiction; the adopted son, the principles of exchange involved in exogamous marriage, the genealogical myths which are invented (not more than half consciously?) to give unity to political units larger than that of the extended family, within which physical kinship is recognized as a matter of fact.

It is also a very ancient trait to recognize that other people look different, and to be curious about this in a pre-scientific way. The Bible contains various myths (which are obscure to me) about the races of man; the art of ancient empires in Egypt and Mesopotamia distinguishes beautifully the traits and physiognomy of captives and of tributary peoples; and the Greek writers of 'histories' (the word then meaning 'inquiries') in the fifth century B.C. began the serious job of creating a biological taxonomy of man.

3. There is an excellent collection of quotations in Chapter 1 of Deutsch (1953).
4. 'I am the root and the offspring of David, and the bright and morning star', *Revelation*, xxii, 16.

Each of these traditions is confused; it is perhaps not very illuminating to explain the nineteenth-century confusion over race as due to their interaction in political rhetoric. But the analogy can be exemplified quite easily:

> And how can man die better
> Than facing fearful odds,
> For the ashes of his fathers,
> And the temples of his Gods ?[5]

Stand with your kindred, do honour to your ancestors, perpetuate your breed.

This happy breed of men, this little world.

And this is still in use, as for instance when someone recently lobbed a bomb into Mr Heath's study, and he remarked that 'nothing the bombers can do would weaken the resolve of the British people to defeat the terrorists. The sooner they learn that we are not that kind of a nation, the fewer lives will be pointlessly lost' (*Glasgow Herald*, 24 December 1974). Perhaps this now has an old-fashioned Churchillian ring, but no one greatly dislikes it.

On the other hand, the pseudo-science of race, once rhetorically powerful, is now universally regarded as disgusting. Or is this merely within the universe of intellectuals? When intellectuals such as John Enoch Powell speak against 'coloured people' they are now careful to avoid the idiom of race and blood, and to substitute references to traditions and culture. But there is probably still (and not only in South Africa) an underlying sentiment, at pre-literate level, that men shaped and coloured differently are not men but animals. There can be no identity between blacks and whites; and there are now radical blacks who proclaim this rhetorically, as well as radically racist whites.

But the 'scientific' rhetoric of race, generated by Victorian theorists, has been effectively killed by modern biology. In the nineteenth century the word 'race' wobbled in significance, including reference to the 'great races of man', black, white,

5. Macaulay, *Lays of Ancient Rome, Horatius*, xxvii.

brown and yellow, to the cult of skull measurements, dolicho-
cephalous, brachycephalous and so on, which generated mythological entities such as Nordic, Alpine and Mediterranean man;
and to the ghosts which haunted comparative philology, in the
shape of Aryan, Turanian, Dravidian and other 'races'. Biological usage now seems settled, in terms of 'the development of
physiological races which eventually become isolated genetically
from the original population'; and in Lewis and Taylor the type
cases are chosen from caprid bugs, apple suckers and eelworms.[6]
That is to say, the word 'race' comes right at the bottom of the
hierarchy of physiological classification; below it comes only a
'population', a more or less bounded group within which there
may develop a 'gene pool' and the characteristics of a 'race'.

There are still some patches of human population in which the
gene pool has been static for many generations. But there must
have been inter-mixture since time immemorial among the
nomads of the great land masses, who met few obstacles to
movement; and this mobility has grown at an increasing pace
through the 'Neolithic revolution' until the coming of modern
industrialism. In consequence, each of the characteristics taken to
distinguish a 'race' of man is spread over a wide span and is not
necessarily associated with other characteristics in a stable way.

What is more, the analysis of genes and blood groups has
added to visible markers of heredity others which can only be
discovered by complex scientific procedures.[7] There are recessive
genes, such as those which determine the incidence of haemo-
philia in men but never in women. There are other genes
associated with diseases in a more complex way, as in the
association between the 'sickle-cell gene' and protection against
malaria. There is very detailed knowledge of the distribution of
genes for different blood groups, and the resulting maps show
both confusion and also areas of relative concentration, which
correspond to what we guess about prehistoric movements of
population.

6. T. Lewis and L. R. Taylor, *Introduction to Experimental Ecology*
(Academic Press, London & New York, 1967), p. 25.

7. J. Z. Young (1971), p. 590 ff.

Hence John Young's conclusion: 'It is doubtful whether strictly "biological" factors in the simple sense are major influences in maintaining the separation of races today' (p. 601). Earlier in the book (Chapter 20) he sketches the complexities of 'The Measurement of Intelligence'. Add these to the complexities of race; mix in the fact that all men are animals specialized in transmission of skills and qualities by culture; add further, that there are localized problems of nutrition and crowding.[8] The only positive conclusion one can reach is that any firm statement about racial traits is rhetoric, not science. It will be interesting to see if response to this strong traditional rhetoric grows weaker in face of the supposed diffusion of scientific culture.

RELIGION

The case of religion is not biological but cultural and semantic. 'Once upon a time' every group had its own gods, spirits, myths and rituals. They were as much a part of life as technology or law or kinship; there was no separate thing called 'religion', though often 'the elders' interviewed by anthropologists talk good sense about the character of myth and its relation to daily life. It was that proto-scientist proto-Marxist Lucretius[9] who stamped on consciousness the recurring refrain;

'Tantum religio potui suadere malorum'

(So great were the evils men learnt from 'religio')

The place of that refrain in the history of thought is clear enough, being part of the rationalism of late Greek philosophy and science.

8. For efforts to disentangle the effects of crowding on human development, see for instance Susan Welch and Alan Booth, 'Crowding as a factor in political aggression: Theoretical aspects and an analysis of some cross-national data': I.P.S.A. Conference Paper (mimeo), 1973.

9. The publication of the student notes Marx made for his thesis on the Greek atomists shows that Marx knew Lucretius well and admired him greatly; Marx/Engels, *Werke*, *Ergänzungsband I* (Berlin, Dietz, 1968), from p. 144 (especially p. 170).

It was only Lucretius who made poetry out of it, and from his poetic examples it is clear that the word *religio* for him meant not 'religion' as we use that word, but something more like 'superstitious credulity'.

Lucretius in fact wrote in a period of the dissolution and re-creation of cultures, of which one part was the genesis of Christianity. In the first centuries A.D. there were a number of 'movements' in the world of the Middle East and Mediterranean, which can be seen retrospectively to have common characteristics; among them a wise man who creates, strives and suffers; a centre of diffusion, but also an appeal to membership without respect of place, history or personal position; a ritual; a body of professional priests; a structure of theological doctrine, assimilated to some extent to philosophical traditions.

Christianity was victorious in the end, after three centuries, against strong rivals recorded in Roman satire and in the crude altars of the frontier legions; Isis, Mithras, Zoroaster, Sol Invictus, and others. No one knows why Christianity was victorious; perhaps because it was more exclusive and demanded exclusive loyalty, perhaps because it had a better form of organization, perhaps because (unlike other Eastern religions) it had a social message for those socially weak (women, children, the poor, the slaves), perhaps because it linked itself to a great philosophical tradition, that of Platonism, and was thus able to enrol intellectuals as well as slaves. Perhaps it was indeed 'the true religion'; however that may be, it became under Constantine the state religion of the Empire, and combined monopoly with a talent for syncretism. Some ancient holy places were destroyed, but many more were built into the new fabric. The West became 'Christendom', a union of secular and religious authority which came near to reestablishing the old unity of custom, belief and worship; and this heritage (though put under siege) was unified rather than dissipated by the military challenge of a rival 'religion'. Islam denied some Christian tenets, but stood out as a phenomenon of the same kind as Christianity.

Christianity, of course, like Islam, has been divided against itself perpetually by schisms and heresies, but none of them was ever dignified by the claim to be 'a new religion'. These two were 'the religions', true and false, until India, South East Asia, China, Japan were brought into contact with Christianity and Islam in the period of European expansion, which laid the world open to European science and philosophy, as the conquests of Alexander had done 1200 years before. There was no longer 'one true religion', except for the professional cadres of Christianity; philosophers and plain men alike were prepared to add to the list of religions as they explored new lands, and sought trade, alliances, and mutual toleration. 'Comparative religion' became an academic subject, and it became necessary to define 'religion'.

A fairly simple (but misleading) distinction could be made between literates and non-literates, those who had 'scriptures' and those who lacked them. The latter were in the end labelled 'animists' and left to the care of missionaries and of social anthropologists. But it was not so easy to deal with 'peoples of the book' (to extend the usual application of that phrase), especially as some of them created strong but diffuse political entities which had no essential 'heart-land' on which to base territorial claims for nationality. This was particularly true for 'John Company', as it explored the problems of managing a commercial empire; in my time it could still be identified, on a tiny scale, as a factor in government in East Africa, where many of the immigrant trading communities, their dhows borne on the monsoon, were diffused along a crescent of coast-line from Mozambique to Java. The situation could be seen on the town plan of Dar-es-Salaam or Mombasa: a place of worship, a social club, a bent towards an economic specialization, sometimes a residential quarter with its own shops, sometimes a strong element of social welfare, sometimes a cricket eleven competing in a league (devised, I suppose, by the imperialists for their own purposes). Of those which I had to learn quickly, because they came to give 'evidence', I remember now the Shia Khoja (orthodox Aga Khan), the Shia Itnasheri (dissidents), the Bohoras, the Baluchis, the Greeks, the Goans, the Somalis, and perhaps one should add the traditional 'Arabs'. From one point of view these were religions, from another they were social and economic organizations, from a third they were states without territories.

This was written large on an enormous scale in India, South East Asia, and East Asia; soldiers and commercial men found their own way through the thicket, 'comparative religion' followed. But it never got nearer to agreement on definition than in another old Latin phrase, *numen inest*;[10] a quotation much in vogue when Western anthropologists believed that all religion grew from 'animism', a belief that there were spirits in all things. Perhaps the Romans were not so insensitive to the intangible as historians and poets have implied:

> And the Romans too have gone at the goose step
> Under a crooked arch into silence.[11]

What is 'numen' except a sense of the special, of the super-human, of awe, of a slight prickling of the hair? Something built into Stonehenge, the Parthenon, the great cathedrals, the Maya pyramids, the ostentatious simplicity of mosques – and even into the ugliness of Welsh chapels.

This large digression may help to place the Orange and the Green; not to belittle them but to lend them dignity. They are the water in which the killers swim, and yet the killers are of an alien species, indeed of several species precariously linked by an obsession with violent death. These have appeared elsewhere in the modern world, and recognize their affinity even amid rivalries. But Green and Orange by contrast have historical depth, each has rituals of binding force (*devoveo*, hence 'devotion'), each has *numen* which repels flippancy.

In other words, I do not know whether or not to classify this factor as 'religion'. But I have no doubt that it is associated far more closely than any other (much more closely than 'race') with individual and social identity, and that such identity can be a political force. Like 'race' it is a force unfashionable among intellectuals, and it is pushed back by secular intellect (*tantum*

10. Ovid, *Fasti*, III. 296.
11. Louis MacNeice, *Blind Fireworks* (Gollancz, 1929), p. 63.

religio . . .) into nooks and crannies of the antique world, such as Ulster.

NATION AND CLASS

There is left a confrontation between nation and class, which has for almost 150 years dominated discussion of political identity. In one sense each of them is now at its zenith. There is little open opposition to the principle that the existence of nationality confers a right to self-government, and that self-government may express itself in a demand for the creation of 'an independent sovereign state'. A few resolute academics (notably Elie Kedourie) stand out against the dogmatism of nationality: a few Western states (notably France towards Basques and Bretons, Spain towards Basques and Catalans) continue to play the nineteenth-century game of assimilation to the culture of the dominant nation within the state. But even Marxist states accept the chosen line of Lenin and Stalin, and grant the premises of nationalism while evading its conclusion. Nationality confers the right to self-government, but no government is legitimate unless led by the 'vanguard of the proletariat', a Communist Party approved by Moscow. This rather crude syncretism of class and nation made it logically possible for Stalin to claim in 1936 that frontier Republics of the Union of Soviet Socialist Republics had the right to secede.[12] With equal cynicism his successors can claim that they are the friends of new nationalities everywhere; and the U.S.A. is trapped into the same commitment by the Soviet line and by its own history, as '*The First New Nation*'[13] 'When in the course of human events, it becomes necessary for one people to dissolve

12. Isaac Deutscher, *Stalin: A Political Biography* (1949; revised ed. Penguin, 1966), p. 378, and Stalin's speech presenting the draft constitution to the 8th Soviet Congress.

13. The title of a book by Seymour Martin Lipset, sub-title, *The United States in Historical and Comparative Perspective* (Basic Books, New York, 1963) which has its own place in the argument about development and identity.

the political bonds which have connected them with another, and to assume among the powers of the earth, the separate and equal station to which the laws of Nature and of Nature's God entitle them . . .'

The consequence has been a multiplication of new states, which pre-supposed new nations. The arithmetic is complex; but roughly a hundred new states have come into being since 1918, and orthodoxy requires that each of these be regarded as a nation state. Many of these states are so weak that they enjoy only an illusory independence, whether controlled by one of the great powers or disputed between them. It is more relevant to the present argument that many of them inherited political leadership from nationalist movements which lacked resources of history, imagination and organization. A few had no indigenous inheritance at all, and merely took over the role of the former expatriate government. 'The state' in such cases can be described pragmatically as a grouping of self-interested individuals, financed and supported diplomatically by external powers. But such a group often follows the traditional rules of the political game; to manoeuvre into a situation of balance which leaves a little leeway for bargaining with their external patrons, to extend internal support (or at least the semblance of it) by playing with the tools described in the next chapter. The state thus seeks to create the nation: but these are sharp weapons, and inexperienced users may cut themselves badly.

Nationalism is universal; nationalism is weak, superficial and frustrated. Yet it continues to attract loyalty and to cost deaths. It is relatively easy to understand the insurgency of the young, and also the conservative instinct to cry 'stop the world I want to get off'. But it beats me to explain why some of the insurgents affirm nationality, others affirm class.

For the concept of class has been under pressure too. Its triumph is apparent. On their own showing, governments based on a Marxist theory of class govern something like one third of mankind; and Marxist oppositions (open or clandestine) are well entrenched in many other states. At the same time Marxism has imposed itself as a political language even on those who are not

Marxists. The theory of neo-colonialism has almost broken loose from a strictly Marxist basis in class analysis, yet it has powerful and relevant things to say about the relations between economic and political power. The story of Allende's Chile, the I.T.T., the C.I.A., the American military, the subservient State Department, the unheeding President adds up to a parable of neo-colonialism. Blind folly, the product of blind forces, led to American confirmation of the neo-colonialist doctrine in an extreme form, and it will not be easy to get back to an analysis in terms of mutual advantage, 'trade and aid'.

Yet class analysis is at present almost as unrealistic as nationalist analysis. The U.S.S.R. has the best disciplined labour force in Europe, a peasantry released from virtual serfdom only at the end of 1960, excellent social services, a career open to those who can climb the educational ladder, a framework of government and management more stable (since Stalin's death) than that of any capitalist country. A worker or his children can share in power only by career advancement into this managerial stratum. How is one to describe this in terms of Marxist class analysis ? The question is not a rhetorical one. There have been times, especially during 'the Patriotic War' against Hitler, when a nationalist analysis made more sense than a class analysis: and there is still talk at times of 'Great Russian chauvinism' on one side, on the other of tendencies towards 'bourgeois nationalism' in the lesser republics. The urban working class has shown none of the class-conscious solidarity and self-confidence shown by the Putilov workers in 1917, East Berlin workers in 1953, Hungarian workers in 1956, Polish workers in December 1970. The urban worker is protected and is preferred, and to that extent it is a workers' state. But it is not a state which grants all power to the workers. To a new bourgeoisie, perhaps ? But this cannot be, since by definition a bourgeois class is one which owns the means of production, distribution, and exchange. Should one, like Djilas, postulate *A New Class?* There is talk of such a managerial class in the West also; defined as a 'class' because it has power without ownership, intermarries within its own circle, and passes advantages to its children which give them a start in the race, the race which is notionally open to all talent. We begin to recognize that an open educational system does not destroy, perhaps enhances, the life chances of the families best organized to handle it, whether it is Russian secondary school, French *lycée*, British comprehensive or American neighbourhood high school. Concerned and able families find their way to the best schools, and transmit to their children a knowledge of how to prosper in that culture. Some well-endowed children reject their differential endowment: but this seems to worry Russian families just as much as it worries parents in France, Britain, and the U.S.A. Some Russian sources admit that the managerial intelligentsia constitutes a stratum but not a class,[14] so as to bring it within the logic of orthodox Marxism; and would claim (not without reason) that it can do nothing without the cooperation of the workers and peasants, who greatly outnumber it.

There seems to be only one escape from these three unconvincing variants, bourgeoisie, New Class, stratum. That is to take refuge in the State and to categorize the U.S.S.R. as 'bureaucracy', applying in rougher Russian conditions Max Weber's grandiose vision of the immaculate (and detestable) rationality of the Prussian system within which he lived his official life. But the 'State' is a term as ambiguous as the term 'class'.[15] The word can refer to a selfish clique of office holders, as Marx described Louis Bonaparte's state in *The Eighteenth Brumaire*. Or the State may comprise the Nation and deserve Burke's description:

> a partnership in all science; a partnership in all art;
> a partnership in every virtue, and in all perfection.[16]

Or it may be a supreme legal entity which formally determines the status of those enrolled within it, in such a way that 4,000 million or so legal persons are partitioned legally (with a trivial

14. A *Zwischenschicht* in the German version of Stalin's speech on the Draft Constitution, 1936.

15. For a fuller discussion, see my *Politics and Social Science* (Penguin, 1967), Chapter 19, pp. 336–40.

16. *Reflections on the Revolution in France* (1790).

number of deviant cases) between some 140 legal units, equal in law but varying in population from 700 million to about 150,000, and almost equally diverse in individual wealth per head. Or (finally) it may be a moral entity, a grand Hegelian category, abstract but forever in search of concrete existence, to be attained through the dialectic of mind and history.

One does not solve any problems of analysis by labelling the system of the U.S.S.R. as 'state capitalism'.

The problem of class analysis is a little easier elsewhere than in the U.S.S.R., in that the complex reality is not fogged by an official statement of orthodoxy. But as a lecturer I am now bored to tears by my own expositions of the orthodoxy of Western social science: class as wealth, class as income, class as way of life, class as job prestige, class as self-rating or 'class-consciousness'. Categorization by class seems simpler if we look back to Marx's time, and imagine the street-scenes shown in old photographs; bourgeoisie and proletariat wear different uniforms; top hat and frock coat, cloth cap and corduroy. And there were also beggars. Nineteenth-century class structure is more clearly visible to us than that of 1976, in which the five indicators I have mentioned so often diverge. The steel erector or deep-sea fisherman earn more than the local branch bank manager or the research scientist. None of them may own 'capital' in the Marxist sense: all may own a house, a car, some insurance policies, some pension rights. All may use the same schools, the same health services, their children may dress alike and talk alike, watch the same telly and listen to the same 'tranny', follow the same teams. The pattern of industrial action now also seems to be 'classless', involving medical consultants, teachers, miners, busmen, sewerage labourers alike, in spite of divergent 'status'. The situation often *feels* more like 'all against all', each in his craft, than like polarization of lesser groups into greater classes dialectically ranged in confrontation.

So too in the U.S.A., Canada, Australasia, perhaps to a greater extent; perhaps to a lesser extent in the countries of old social hierarchy and old European Marxism, in particular France, Germany and Italy.

But there are three factors which bring us back to the predominance of class analysis. The first is history. If Marx and Engels had both died young, we should nevertheless have written the social and economic history of the last four centuries in terms of social and economic class. Scholars who were not also revolutionaries might have paid more attention to deviant cases (which are often the most illuminating); but Marx was indomitable in gathering data, and the data demanded these overriding generalizations. I write in the next chapter about history as myth: scholarly history may reinforce history as myth, and this comes home to most of us if we have the curiosity to trace our great-grandparents and to seek to place them in the context of their time. Each of us could tell a tale in terms of class position, class differentiation, class mobilization.

The second is that what I have written about the entangled and overlapping structures of the 'post-industrial state' concentrates on the great majority in the middle. If we shift our eyes to the 10 per cent 'rich', the 10 per cent 'poor' we get a different feeling for the situation. It is a pity that the Left concentrate on salaries gross of tax as indicators of wealth and prestige. Tax (if deducted at source or paid promptly and scrupulously) is a great leveller, and a salary of (say) £30,000 would on that basis not pay for more than a modest Victorian standard of house, servants, and education. But there are those who live conspicuously[17] far above that standard; partly through 'expense account living', partly because there are those who live not from income but from the manipulation of capital. A very diverse crew – great families, great speculators, a few independent industrialists, a few managers rewarded by a share of the equity, and diverse eccentrics like one-shot inventors, pools winners and pop-stars.

There has been little social research in that area; but the problems of poverty attract more attention. We now know where to look; single-parent families, especially if burdened with problems of physical or mental ill health; those dependent on the

17. cf. Veblen's 'laws of conspicuous waste': *The Theory of the Leisure Class* (1899; Allen & Unwin, 1970), p. 118.

lowest-paid jobs, and no overtime; the elderly, if they have no comfort from an 'extended family'; the marginals who are on the line between low-paid jobs and unemployment – physically handicapped, educationally backward, alcoholic, mentally unstable. We have no adequate statistical measures; and the isolation of individuals may be more heart-breaking than a supposed 'culture of poverty'. These people are too weak to be classed, even as *lumpenproletariat*.

But in non-statistical terms the top 10 per cent and the bottom 10 per cent colour our thinking about the system. The contrast remains intolerable, even though it has little to do with Marxist class analysis. Some of the big spenders may be by some indicators 'proletarian': some of the half-starved may be by the same indicators cast-offs of the bourgeoisie. One sense of our supposed 'social contract' is that this contrast must be abolished, as it was in time of war, before we can put our minds to the problems of justice and cooperation among those whom Harold Wilson once called 'the useful people'.

The third factor is that of the so-called 'external proletariat'; more exactly, the fact that unless we choose to ignore information we are now well-informed about poverty in the world. We can of course fiddle a bit with the statistical returns. For instance, they contain no credit item for sunlight and warmth in the tropics which could not be bought in northern countries for less than (to put it modestly) £1000 a year per man, woman and child. They draw attention to the problem of assessing the cash value of subsistence farming, and of the farm background of many of the urban poor, as a kind of resource in extreme trouble. But mitigate the figures as you will, the fact remains that about one third of mankind lie not on the poverty line but on the subsistence line. We protect them against population control by killing epidemics; they have no one (except for some threadbare illiterate gods) to protect them from under-nutrition and possible starvation.

Is this the 'exploitation' of a proletariat by a bourgeoisie, which would include even our poorest if we judged class in terms of cash income? Personally I find the alternative formulation even less attractive; that (as some American sociologist wrote about urban negroes in the 1960s) the very poor are 'functionally superfluous'. In other words, they yield no surplus to exploit; the balance of wealth would be the same even if they vanished; wealth would not be lost – merely people.

I feel that these three factors sustain class as a concept of power, in spite of all that is written about the failure of the predicted class polarization in the West. It is no wonder that there arise among Marxist factions different views about analysis and about tactics, views often morally attractive and of high intellectual quality. But, taught by the experience of a century, one has learnt to suspect that in some *groupuscules* genuine members and agents of different intelligence services attend in about equal numbers. I am not sure that police spies and *agents provocateurs* are spotted by young European revolutionaries more readily now than they were in the days of *The Secret Agent* and *Under Western Eyes*.[18]

As in earlier sections of this chapter, I have written as if to discredit nation and class, and I have perhaps been drawn a little way from the main point, which was that the Victorian writers discerned four powerful intermediaries in the creation of a thing that might well be called 'political identity'. These were race, religion, nation, class. I think I have shown that (on quite distinct grounds) neither race nor religion can now be regarded as important, in the Victorian sense of those words. This does not mean that the words and their referents now have no emotive charge. But in each case there is a gap between intellectual perceptions and those of plain traditional people – the saloon-bar talkers.

As regards nation and class the case is different. These terms retain their power over all of us: they may be taken in rather different senses by intellectuals and by plain men, but they can-

18. 1907 and 1911; this is Conrad writing not as a sea-captain, but as a son of Polish gentry.

not be thrown into a conversation anywhere in the Western world without (metaphorically) exploding it. They move men emotionally: a few of them they move to action. I am afraid these few do not wait for intellectuals to clarify their concepts.

Of course, the fifth element in J. S. Mill's analysis was that of 'common language'. This the Marxist class analysis deliberately ignored, in spite of all that Marx had to suffer in multi-lingual meetings of revolutionaries. In a sense Marxists sought to create a new common language for the revolution, and they did not fail completely. But it is odd that Stalin, for whom ideology was always subordinate to tactics, was the only Marxist of his generation to put language in a central position in his analysis.[19]

19. 'Marxism and Linguistics' (1950), translated and republished in Bruce Franklin (ed.), *The Essential Stalin: Major Theoretical Writings, 1905–52* (Croom Helm, 1973).

CHAPTER 15

HOW TO DO THINGS WITH WORDS

All speech is a form of customary behavior, but, likewise, all customary behavior is a form of speech, a mode of communicating information. In our dress, in our manners, even in our most trivial gestures, we are constantly 'making statements' that others can understand. For the most part the statements refer to human relationships and to status.

E. R. LEACH: Article on 'Ritual' in the *Encyclopaedia of the Social Sciences* (David L. Gills (ed.), The Macmillan Co. and the Free Press, 1968), Vol. 13, p. 523.

'THUS perhaps nine tenths of the people of England say "I'se do't" instead of "I will do it", but no gentleman would use that expression without the imputation of vulgarity.'

ADAM SMITH, *Rhetoric and Belles Lettres*, J. M. Lothian, ed., Nelson, 1963, p. 2. (The sage gives himself away. 'Will' for 'shall' used to be labelled a scotticism.)

I HAVE now pursued the concept of social identity through four chapters, dealing respectively with the grammar of the first person, singular and plural; with the psychologists' attempts to pin down the concept of 'identification with . . .'; with what seem practical identities, shared interest and shared location; with the classification of four types of cultural identity, bequeathed to us by the nineteenth century – nation, race, religion, class.

These last three chapters have been somewhat sceptical but not dismissive. The metaphor 'to ensnare a concept' is imperfect, since in this sort of hunting one does not know what one's prey is till one has caught it; or perhaps it still slips away as one gets closer. But readers expect and deserve a report on the state of play.

In this chapter, then, I discuss language in an extended sense, for three reasons. Firstly, because in Chapter 10 I discuss politics in terms of common purpose, and conscious concerted action is not conceivable without channels of communication. Secondly, because though Chapter 11 on the personal pronouns is amateurish, it seems to offer more scope than the voluminous branches of academic knowledge referred to in the next three chapters. Thirdly, in the spirit of the late John Austin, speaking in 1956, 'Is it not possible that the next century may see the birth, through the joint labours of philosophers, of grammarians, and numerous other students of language, of a true and comprehensive *science of language*?' (John Austin's italics).[1] That is to say, the topics set out in the last three chapters seem to look backwards, to nineteenth-century psychology, economics, geography, political science; the topic of language in an extended sense ('How to talk: some simple ways', another of Austin's jesting titles)[2] seems to me to be the subject of fertile work in many disciplines here and now, and to be open-ended, to be working ahead into new ground.

But I put this forward only as prolegomena, in terms of another quotation from John Austin. 'You've got to get something on your plate before you can start messing it around!'[3] This is what I have on my plate, and now I can start. But of course I cannot conclude; I wish to suggest inquiry, not to impose conclusions.

Probably most people still think of a language (even 'one's native language') as something that exists in books and is taught from books. There are some mutters of opposition, demanding the de-schooling of language, and questioning whether there is any point in learning spelling and grammar; people got along very well without them before writing was invented; and even thereafter, it was some time before academic grammarians imposed the strict discipline of 'orthography'. There is probably a case to be made for standardizing written language, but not

---

1. In the British Academy lecture on 'Ifs and Cans', *Philosophical Papers* (ed. Urmson and Warnock, Clarendon Press, 1961), p. 180.

2. At p. 181 of that collection.

3. *Sense and Sensibilia* (ed. G. J. Warnock, Clarendon Press, 1962), p. 142.

necessarily in the present form and not so that it imposes a class barrier between those who write 'correctly' and those who merely write intelligibly.

But to write language down, though it has had revolutionary social effects, was no more than a spin-off from language in its natural habitat, that of speech, the mouths of men:[4] even today, speech is many times more plentiful than writing, and perhaps it is even gaining on it, with the support of telephone and tape recorder. It is at least fifty years now since the study of language turned away from the formalism of comparative grammar (which had been a great thing in its day), as Browning fixed it for us in 'A Grammarian's Funeral':

> He settled Hoti's business – let it be! –
> Properly based *Oun* –
> Gave us the doctrine of the enclitic *De*,
> Dead from the waist down.

In a sense, a turn away from an old formalism is a turn towards a new formalism, since the object of a scientific quest is first to find, then to explain, a repetitive pattern in things. But the turn away from structure to speech, from *langue* to *parole*, in Saussure's terminology,[5] created, by a kind of Copernican revolution, a new field of study and a new attitude to it. Actors (those 'hypocrites', in Greek) have always known about patterns of speech and gesture; and the ancient study of rhetoric to some extent formalized this knowledge and made it the basis of a liberal education. Rhetoric has left some traces in our education; quite reasonably, the first known chair of politics was founded at Uppsala in the seventeenth century as a chair of rhetoric and political science. But rhetoric as a formal academic subject had virtually died out by the end of the eighteenth century, and the teaching of communication and persuasion, of establishing

4. A Latin poet's epitaph on himself: 'Let no one mourn me; "I shall be alive, fluttering upon the mouths of men"' (volito vivus per ora virium); Ennius, Merry *Selected Fragments* (Clarendon Press, 1898), p. 67.

5. John Lyons, *Introduction to Theoretical Linguistics* (Cambridge University Press, 1969), p. 51.

identity with an audience, has had to begin again, and has by no means yet regained its key position among the social sciences.

Perhaps one could describe this move outwards from the formalism of orthography and grammar as being an expansion in three dimensions: downwards, sideways and upwards. This is crude, but perhaps excusable in an unprofessional summary. All three dimensions are important to the understanding of politics.

DIALECTS, ACCENTS, IDIOLECTS

By movement downwards I mean the process of research which goes behind the standardized forms of writing and speech, which are mainly products of the seventeenth and eighteenth centuries. Historically, standard English was imposed on an ancient structure of local variants. For instance, the late medieval 'Scottish' tongue, extending into northern England, might conceivably have achieved a separate standing as a written language if politics and power had gone that way – probably written Scots was, at the parting of the ways, at least as distinct from southern English as Norwegian was from Danish, when Norway became separate in 1814. English in fact sustained its unity, as a written language, but till quite recently the regional variants survived as dialects, spoken by all classes, though the higher social classes were generally bi-lingual, in that they wrote in 'standard', could switch between 'standard' and 'dialect' according to the social context of conversation.[6] This bi-lingualism created poets in the written dialect (Burns is a key example, but the Scots dialect was not unique in this respect), and poetic dialect (the Doric) became 'respectable' in a rather pedantic way, in that ancient Greek poets had to some extent been able to switch between written dialects according to genre and metre form.

6. There is an article by A. R. Townsend and C. C. Taylor ('Regional Culture and Identity in Industrialized Societies: the case of North-East England', *Regional Studies*, 9 [1975], p. 379) which uses the self-assessment of respondents ('with what accent do you speak yourself?') as a measure of relatively strong or weak 'regional identity'. Cf. Peter Trudgill, *The Social Differentiation of English in Norwich* (Cambridge University Press, 1974).

The sharp edges of dialect have now been eroded down to the level of accent: but native English speakers are intensely sensitive to this from childhood. When I was at school in Edinburgh I used to think that I could by accent pin a class-mate down as residing in perhaps one square mile of a city of perhaps forty square miles. I exaggerated; and in any case the ear grows dull with age. But changing patterns of speech mirror changing patterns of society and politics. Britain between the wars was governed by the Oxford accent of the Tories in face of the regional accents of the Labour Party; and the B.B.C. in the early days of radio insisted on the B.B.C. accent – the announcers wore dinner jackets when on duty. From 1926 there existed an eminent and very argumentative Advisory Committee on Spoken English. The break came during the war, when Wilfred Pickles, a Yorkshire character actor, was brought down from Manchester to London to become a regular news reader.[7] There was a storm of protest, but it passed, and one can now deduce that traces of regional accent are positively welcome, provided that they are compatible with clarity.[8] Perhaps in its claim to be truly national the Conservative Party has been handicapped by the present prevalence within it of 'the Oxford accent', once the badge of natural and inherited ascendancy. Certainly in Scotland the Tories have contributed to their present difficulties by wiping out the old urban 'progressives'; an ill-disciplined lot of selfish local bourgeoisie, quite generally disliked in their native habitat. But now the only survivor of them, among sixteen Tory M.P.s, is Teddy Taylor of Cathcart; he speaks the language, therefore he is neither laird nor lawyer, and perhaps he is now the only Tory politician who carries any personal weight in Scotland.[9]

7. Yet in the T.V. series *Word of Mouth* (B.B.C. 2, August–September 1976) Melvyn Bragg set off the accent of the Scottish Establishment against other Scottish voices and he did not do the same for England, as we had expected. The B.B.C.'s old worry about the voice of Royalty?

8. Asa Briggs, *The History of Broadcasting in the United Kingdom* (Oxford University Press, 3 Vols.: Vol. 1 [1961], p. 292; Vol. 2 [1965], pp. 16, 40, 467–9; Vol. 3 [1970], p. 59).

9. At last recognized by Mrs Thatcher as spokesman on Scotland, December 1976.

One can carry this level of analysis further down the scale to the level of individual competitors for leadership. Winston Churchill constructed for himself an absolutely unique speaking voice based partly on the speech defects of his childhood, partly on his concept of the actor's part he had written for himself (de Gaulle did likewise, perhaps learning a little from Churchill). Harold Wilson's accent and its fluctuations might perhaps be traced from old tape recordings; it seems now to have settled to a kind of diffuse regionalism (or 'Mummerset') which is in accord with his image of the sort of man he wishes to appear to be. It would be interesting to try to measure reactions to Heath's speaking voice in different parts of the country. To my ear, in the North, it sounded like a brave but not quite perfect effort to superimpose 'upper-class speech' on a rather flat, local, south-eastern accent; that is to say, it attempted to speak with the voice of traditional authority, and it failed. This interpretation is no more than a hunch; the point is that 'identification with' and 'identification who' are much influenced by accent and by personal speech (the voice-print is as unique as the fingerprint).

There is also more general identification based on the survival of older forms of speech. Welsh and Scottish accents have been fair game since Shakespeare's time. Now we can add West Indian and Indo-Pak speech, as specified by Spike Milligan and other mimics. And we know a bit about 'Strine', and we tend to find rather offensive the overtones of Afrikaans in South African English, even though the accent is shared by black and brown South Africans.

One step further, and one is involved in the study of *lingua franca*, trade languages, pidgins. These are more strange to us, but not without political significance in some parts of the world: for instance, the linguistic zone of Kiswahili in East and Central Africa, spreading across the frontiers of new states: and the extraordinary case of Neo-Melanesian, once regarded as a comic pidgin, now the official written language of one of the newest states, New Guinea, lately emerged from the stone age.[10]

10. And in the West Indies and Surinam also; see Peter Trudgill, *Sociolinguistics: An Introduction* (Penguin, 1974).

BODILY EXPRESSION

By extension sideways I mean the realization that 'speaking' is not done only with voice and breath. J. L. Austin was concerned more abstractly with 'how to do things with words'; in particular, he emphasized speech as *act*, and in doing so dethroned the statement (subject-verb-predicate) as 'queen of the battlefield' in grammar and in logic. The statement, when it comes out, is important, and is often marked as such. But in the flow of speech statements are only one element, and many apparent statements are pseudo-statements at best. 'Fine day today'. 'Quite'.

Independently of this philosophic point, and to some extent independently of one another, various observers have begun to look at the bodily movements which accompany the flow of speech and the intervals between speech. There is Erving Goffman on *The Presentation of Self in Everyday Life*; Ray Birdwhistell on a new subject called 'kinesics' which deals with the movements and facial expressions which accompany talk;[11] Michael Argyle,[12] studying the pattern of 'conversational behaviour' in laboratory conditions; Eibl-Eibesfeldt[13] photographing facial expressions and gestures throughout the world, and seeking for evidence that certain forms of expression are older than speech, are genetically transmitted, and are akin to the 'self-presentation' of the higher mammals.

A blind man can hear and understand speech though he cannot see the speaker. A deaf man can see the speaker and up to a a point can see speech; try T.V. with the sound off, as a first approach.

This is what the old rhetoricians called *actio*, the visual presentation of speech; and they had relevant things to say which 'the born actor' learns for himself. This is another thing that politicians must learn, often with reference to different media

11. *Kinesics and Context: Essays on Body-Motion Communication* (1970; Penguin 1973).

12. *Social Interaction* (Methuen, 1969).

13. I. Eibl-Eibesfeldt: *Love & Hate: On the Natural History of Basic Behaviour Patterns*, translated by G. Strachan (Methuen, 1971).

and to audiences grouped in different patterns – the mass rally, and the fireside talk. The sight of Hitler speaking was as devastating as the voice. Not for nothing was he called 'carpet-biter'.

But I cannot at present see much in this for political discovery, once the point is taken that we are all, and this includes politics at all levels, not only talkers but also performers.

MYTH, SYMBOL, RITUAL, IDEOLOGY

Finally, the extension of language study upwards, and by this I mean that the concept of 'common language', of identity through language, is not restricted to words, but includes also 'things' more general than words, which can be used to speak powerfully at higher levels than those of social chat and instrumental cooperation. I summarize these as myth, symbol, ritual and ideology, and I believe them to be of extreme importance in the attempt to give a workable meaning to talk about social and political 'identity'.

There is nothing new about the study of these 'things' (it is difficult to find a generic word for them, since words such as 'concepts' or 'ideas' are too specific). What is relatively new is to assimilate them to the idea of language, basing this on the perception that a 'common language' involves sharing words and also at a 'higher' level sharing 'things' which lie behind words. Sometimes an attempt is made to say these things explicitly, but this is generally imperfect. They are said indirectly and by implication in much serious talk; they are stored in memory, often sub-consciously; they may be 'acted out'. These memories and these performances lift up and intensify the shared social content of language.

There is a very large literature of these topics, myth, symbol, ritual and ideology;[14] and its boundaries are not easy to settle because this area is not separated by clear frontiers from the

14. This is not as well known to political scientists as it should be and I include a list of Further Reading as an appendix.

bordering territories of rhetoric and style. There is certainly something in the point taken by Roland Barthes,[15] that there is a road to understanding society through the arts of speech and writing which has a right to claim parity with the route through social science. It is extravagant to write that:

> In contrast to the integral truth of literature, the human sciences, belatedly formulated in the wake of bourgeois positivism, appear as the technical alibis proffered by our society in order to maintain within itself the fiction of a theological truth proudly, and improperly, freed from language.

But extravagance (as Barthes is very well aware) is itself a trick of rhetoric; and rhetoric is surely an integral part of politics. Barthes's invention of the term 'writing' (*écriture*) as 'an *idiolect*, an individual's choice of a mode, style or attitude, which is appropriate to his biological self, acceptable to his society . . . partly conditioned, partly a free choice', is clearly relevant to the discussion of 'identity', individual and social. But such a study expands till it becomes a study of all human communication, and its 'idiolects'. In fact, it is not feasible here, and perhaps not feasible for social scientists at all, in that their tools are not sharp enough for the task. There are limited areas within which the measurement of literary style is feasible and illuminating, and this is true also of political style and political culture. But it is also necessary to have some understanding of the whole setting within which political communication takes place, the language of politics in an extended sense. It is as hard to 'learn' this as to learn to speak a natural language, and neither operation can readily be defined as a 'scientific' one. To put it another way, machine translation of natural language has proved baffling to computer scientists; and so also with political language.

I thought at first that I could abbreviate this discussion and give it some rigour by appealing to standard dictionaries and to the old and new *Encyclopaedias of the Social Sciences*, 1932 and

15. From an article by Barthes in *The Times Literary Supplement* of 28 September 1967, quoted by Tom Buchan, 'Writing versus Literature', *Scottish International, April 1968*, p. 17.

1968. But the result merely illustrates the difficulties, partly in that dictionaries differ, partly in that myth, symbol and ritual are regularly treated as words mutually defined in a circular way; and the circle sometimes extends to include 'ideology', although that has generally been treated quite separately by academics. For instance the *Random House Dictionary* (1966) defines 'ideology' as 'the body of doctrine, myth, symbol, etc. of a social movement, institution, class or large group'. Clearly, there has also been change over time, particularly in regard to discussion of 'ideology': the 1932 *Encyclopaedia* does not find it worth an article; that of 1968 gives it two articles and forty columns, far more than Myth, Symbol and Ritual together. Indeed the new *Encyclopaedia* lumps Myth and Symbol together, in a single article by Victor Turner, and gives Symbol no separate treatment. Turner's special interest is in Ritual: but that earns a separate article by Edmund Leach, whose special interest is in Myth.

The argument over T. S. Kuhn's 'paradigm' of normal science has brought the word 'paradigm' into some disrepute; a critic has detected 'not less than twenty-one different senses in his book, possibly more, not less',[16] and Kuhn is now himself very cautious. Nevertheless, let us start with a paradigm, that of the Christian Eucharist, and remember that what follows is written without reference to truth or falsehood, belief or disbelief. There is an exceptionally powerful myth, that of the whole Gospel narrative, into which is set an explicit instruction about ritual and symbol:

And he took bread, and gave thanks, and brake it, and gave unto them, saying, This is my body, which is given for you: this do in remembrance of me:
Likewise also the cup after supper, saying. This cup is the new testament in my blood, which is shed for you.

(*Luke*, xxii, 19, 20)

16. What's more, she lists them: Margaret Masterman, 'The Nature of a Paradigm', in Imre Lakatos and Alan Musgrave (eds.), *Criticism and the Growth of Knowledge* (Cambridge University Press, 1970).

The ritual perpetuates the story, the story explains the ritual, the ritual involves believers as active participants, the symbols abbreviate or condense or encapsulate the whole 'meaning' of these acts of participation.

Take by way of contrast and confirmation the speech of one of the women in Aristophanes' *Lysistrata*: they have declared a sex strike and have allied with the enemy's women to enforce peace between the men. She begins (I paraphrase):

> Citizens, what we have to say is to the city's advantage. And so it should be. The city reared me in splendour and delight. When I was seven, I was train-bearer to the Goddess, when I was ten I ground flour for the hallowed bread, then I was a little bear, dressed in a tawny tunic at the Brauronia; when I was a young woman and beautiful I carried a basket at the Panathenaia, wreathed with ripe figs.
> Am I not then bound to speak for the city's good? Don't grudge to listen, simply because I am a woman. I live under the same sky as you, and I pay my taxes too – the lives of my sons.

The point is that the bawdy fun stops dead for a moment: Aristophanes softens the audience with four quick references to symbols which they all knew (and it takes the commentators volumes to explain them), and then hits straight at the tragic paradox of women and war. And so back to farce: 'What right have you to grunt? If you get in my way I'll bash your jaw with this platform shoe, a new one for today.'

Myth, ritual and symbol woven together to establish identity with the audience, and to soften it for a blow which it cannot parry.

And here is another example, from a 'travel talk' about gypsies in the small, French town of Saintes-Maries-de-la-Mer, which I include because it seems to be untainted by academic comment.

> On the Thursday, when the fun has temporarily died down, the effigy of Saint Sara is brought out of its crypt and placed on a platform where her face gradually turns pink under the hundreds of kisses given in homage by the gipsies. A member of each family wraps a silken

cloth about her in memory of the clothes she stole 2000 years ago,[17] turning her finally into a shapeless bundle of fabric.

The next day, the saint is carried jubilantly through the town, preceded by a company of *gardiens* and escorted by a choir of girls in Provençal dresses, singing chants of a past age, while the *gitans* bring up the rear of the procession with shouts of 'Sara . . . Sara'.

When at last the procession reaches the burning sands and the *gardiens* have ridden their horses into the sea until the waves break over the animals' flanks, the ritual reaches its climax. The litter upon which the saint has been borne is carried over the water while screaming gipsies splash Sara's multi-coloured garments with sea-water.

There is a final outburst of joy, the litter is turned round, and the procession makes its way back to the town, escorting the saint back to her gloomy crypt. By the following morning, most of the visitors have already left on their stateless wanderings, and Saintes-Maries-de-la-Mer resumes its year-long slumber.[18]

Is ideology then irrelevant to these pre-logical or meta-logical instruments of solidarity ? The word has had an unlucky history. It began as a perfectly good text-book word in the 1790s; in philosophy, there would be a section on ideology, about ideas within the mind, a section on phenomenology, the impact of appearances on the mind. But then Napoleon talked of *idéologues* as idle wind-bags, Marx irrevocably linked the word with alienation and false consciousness. In consequence, it is very hard now to get the word back into neutral, as the *Shorter Oxford Dictionary* (corrected to 1959) attempts to do; 'A system of ideas concerning phenomena, especially those of social life; the manner of thinking characteristic of a class or an individual.'

But I should like to do so, if possible, because I can see two distinct problems of 'ideology'. One of them is that of 'false consciousness', which surely must involve hypocrisy; granted, there is a further twist, that the hypocrite may not be aware of

17. She is said to have stolen food and clothing for the two 'Saintes Mairies' who were shipwrecked here after the crucifixion.

18. By John D. Berbiers, *Glasgow Herald*, 1 May 1976. Professor V. W. Turner has been working on 'pilgrimages' (see his *Dramas, Fields and Metaphors*, Cornell University Press, 1974) as rituals of liminality. This naïve story fits his concepts very well.

his or her hypocrisy, may not be in a historical situation in which such awareness would be possible at all, except for a very gifted person. But such hypocrisy need not be logical in form; there are hypocrites of ritual, myth and symbol also.

The scribes and Pharisees sit in Moses' seat . . .
But all their words they do for to be seen of men: they make broad their phylacteries, and enlarge the borders of their garments.
And love the uppermost rooms at feasts, and the chief seats in the synagogues,
And greetings in the markets, and to be called of men, Rabbi, Rabbi . . .
Woe unto you, scribes and Pharisees, hypocrites! for ye are like unto whited sepulchres, which indeed appear beautiful outward, but are within full of dead men's bones, and of all uncleanness. (*Matthew*, xxiii, 2–7, 27)

A class which has survived beyond the period of its historical function is in its nature exposed to the risk of hypocrisy and false consciousness.

The other sense of ideology, recognized in the dictionaries, but now eroded, is that of 'doctrine', the attempt to ground logically and to expound systematically the meaning of a complex of myth, ritual and symbol; to explain rationally man's position in the universe. I talk of rationality, not of science, because it is by all ordinary criteria of science impossible for a man scientifically to get outside the universe and to state his position in relation to it. By definition, if one stands outside the universe all points of reference and orientation have gone. An exercise on this scale requires some fulcrum which is extralogical. But, equally, the objects of faith are insecure without a grounding in explicit and consistent explanation. Doctrine (to use a word less loaded than is ideology) has a place in social experience and justification, even at quite simple levels. Lysistrata's creator dare not over-burden his audience: but her case for peace could if necessary be stated in axioms and syllogisms. In Victor Turner's[19] studies

19. *The Ritual Process: Structure and Anti-Structure* (Routledge & Kegan Paul, 1969; Pelican edition, 1974).

of ritual among the pre-literate Ndembu of Zambia did not lack
the help of 'religious specialists' (p. 9) who could offer 'interpretation' and 'exegesis' of the ritual texts and actions; and he
adds that 'the interpretations were, on the whole, mutually consistent' and 'might be said to constitute the standardized
hermeneutics of Ndembu culture, rather than the free associations or eccentric views of individuals'.

In fact, the Ndembu, though rich in ritual and symbol, are not
rich in mythology about gods. So it would be ironical to call this
their 'theology'. But this is the doctrine of their ritual, and it is
one which Victor Turner handles and explores until he elicits
from it a doctrine for which he claims universal validity as an
implication of man's life in society; the doctrine that in all social
organization there arise dilemmas because of incompatibility
between structured hierarchical organization and *communitas*, the
simple doctrine of the poem Auden rejected, 'we must love one
another or die'.[20] Turner quotes (p. 6) from Monica Wilson:[21]

Rituals reveal values at their deepest level ... men express in ritual
what moves them most, and since the form of expression is convention-
alized and obligatory, it is the values of the group that are revealed. I
see in the study of rituals the key to an understanding of the essential
constitution of human societies.

Both these authors, and many others, have been in search of
such an 'essential constitution', and it is in this area we must
search for that elusive thing, 'social and political identity'. But
I feel bound to add that we need also what Turner himself
supplies, the doctrine latent in the ritual. The founding of the
Last Supper was also a doctrinal or theological event. Its founder
was himself a Rabbi, and all his acts and words have relevance to
an ancient doctrinal context of a very complex kind. But he chose
– and the Gospel authors portray this – another mode of expression, a more powerful one for his purpose, because the capacity

20. See the *Listener*, 1977, p. 419 and p. 699; the line is not to be found in
Auden's collected poems.
21. Monica Wilson, 'Nyakyusa ritual and symbolism'; *American Anthropologist*, 56 (1954), p. 241.

to understand doctrine and to debate in terms of doctrine is specialized and stratified. All Ndembu take part in rituals, and all can feel what Turner expresses for them (p. 43): 'The symbolic expression of group concern for an unfortunate individual's welfare, coupled with the mobilization of a battery of "good" things for her benefit, and the conjunction of the individual's fate with symbols of cosmic processes of life and death – do these really add up for us to something merely "unintelligible"?' The risk of course is that doctrine may be rarefied, specialized, stratified; alien to the rank and file. And so it has often been; the *profanum vulgus*, the unhallowed public, must be excluded from the holiest places of ritual and doctrine. One must face the fact that Christian theology has had a bad record historically; that the doctrine of the Last Supper has furnished ideology (or dogma) for war between Christian sects. But the choice (to my mind) is not open; men are creatures who 'act out' their internal stress, but they also ask questions such as 'Why?' and 'How?', and they accept answers in various different styles. One of these styles is scientific: another is doctrinal or ideological, or even 'dogmatic'. Both styles lead in the end to unanswered, perhaps unanswerable, questions: but scientific answers (though relative) at least seek to be free of context; ideological answers are bound to the social context in which they are given, and to that extent 'identify it', and are 'identified with' it.[22]

I am therefore quite well content to accept the word 'identity' in the context of language in the extended sense which has been sketched here. Language as stated in grammars must in life be extended downwards to dialects, accents, and idiosyncrasies of speech; sideways to include ways in which we communicate intelligibly alongside words and between words; upwards to include the grandiose complexities and practical simplicities of ideology, myth, ritual and symbol. This is 'how to talk' and we share with one another in 'talk'. This is 'shared identity'; shar-

22. One could spin a long tale about the meanings of ideology, doctrine, dogma, in different languages and different cults. But that, as Kipling would have put it, is another story.

ing in a most peculiar abstract something-or-other, but nevertheless 'sharing', in that the thing makes no sense except as something common to human beings, in dyads, triads, groups and
multitudes. The community of communicators, vague though it
is, is yet sharper in definition than community of interest and
contiguity in space (Chapter 14). The traditional concepts of our
modern world, nation, race, religion, class retain their positions
of power: but each can be generalized most effectively in terms
of an exchange of, or participation in, symbolic satisfactions.
This is not merely a point of theory, it is a point of practice also;
we shall understand better, we shall manipulate (and resist
manipulation) most effectively, if we try to learn more of what
goes on around us in the four mutually defining dimensions of
myth, symbol, ritual and ideology.

CHAPTER 16

POSTSCRIPT

THIS book has presented a serious argument in what may seem a trivial way, provoked by the familiar process of the erosion of the meaning of a word which had once a rich and subtle range.

The present use of 'political identity' seems merely to by-pass problems raised by stronger and more traditional words, such as honour, pride, loyalty, comradeship, and self-awareness of these.

Nevertheless, I have found for myself that 'personal identity' denotes a set of problems which have troubled Western poets, novelists and philosophers since the dawn of the romantic movement, and that nothing could have prevented the spill-over by analogy of 'personal identity' into 'collective identity'. My problem therefore was to put 'political' or 'collective identity' in a better context than that from which it sprang, a not very successful American project on a not very precise topic, that of 'political development'. I have illustrated the cross-currents linking American, French and German thought; and the theme is now dominant in the United Kingdom.

The argument carried me through a sequence of stages to the four linked concepts, myth, symbol, ritual and ideology; and I stand by the conclusion that these are now and always have been necessary (though not perhaps sufficient) tools in the process of political analysis.

But two questions arise which deserve at least a provisional response: first, that of philosophical difficulties, secondly that of empirical study.

I am to the best of my ability writing in order to evade philosophical difficulties and controversies. One of these is the puzzle about 'private languages'. We talk to ourselves, of course, in all senses of the word 'talk', even including that of facial expression and gesticulation. But can we talk to ourselves except

in a 'public language'? Is the concept of language not primarily
social? Is not our self-consciousness itself an aspect of society?
Is 'the private man' even conceivable or expressible? All that
need be said is that in the present field of discussion two things
are inseparable; the public 'language' which constitutes shared
identity, the 'idiolect' or individual style which is for each man
unique (though of course it can be analysed and exposed by the
conscious mimic, and can be copied unawares by those within a
circle of influence).

There is a second philosophical point about the mutual entail-
ment of myth, ritual, symbol and doctrine. How do I envisage
these 'things' and their inter-relation? Can it be defined more
specifically in words? Can it be 'operationalized'? That would
be a fair challenge, but this is not the place to respond to it
formally. I note only one point, as being of direct relevance in
practical analysis. It is hard, perhaps impossible, to treat any
one of the four in isolation. Nevertheless, one must be prepared
to admit that the mix varies for different peoples and at different
historical periods. The Ndembu (writes Turner)[1] are weaker
than some other African tribes in myth, but their neighbours
recognize that they are very good at ritual, which includes a
particularly rich and varied use of symbolism. In handling
doctrine they (or at least their specialists) are of course naïve and
limited as compared with the theologians and ideologists of great
religions and movements; nevertheless they possess a logical and
consistent 'hermeneutic'. Other pre-literate peoples may be
relatively poor in ritual, and yet rich in mythology: it would be a
commonplace to say that the early Greeks excelled in myth, the
early Romans in ritual. Similarly the mix may vary at different
periods within one civilization. At present our theologians are
rich in doctrine but quite isolated from the mass. Grass-root
religions spring up continually in the present age on the margins
of traditional 'churches', Christian, Moslem, Buddhist, Hindu.
They are often stronger than the great religions in capacity to
bind their members together ritually, yet their doctrines are
derivative and impoverished. Daniel Bell was unlucky enough to

1. *The Ritual Process*, pp. 4–5 and elsewhere.

publish at the end of the 1950s a volume of essays called *The End of Ideology: On the Exhaustion of Political Ideas in the Fifties*;[2] the 1960s were, as it turned out, a decade in which the Western world (including the Marxist states) were driven by stress to endless ideological debate, a phase which still continues. Or perhaps doctrinal debate was 'the opiate of the intellectuals': the masses reacted less sensitively to the stress of 'future shock'. Or perhaps there was an intensification of neurotic violence; a spread of the drug culture; an increase in the birth-rate of religious sects (*groupuscules* for the intellectuals, *ashrams* for the drop-outs)? But there is no technique available that can measure these trends reliably.

It seems therefore that we have in this field a task which is not easy to handle with the approved techniques of social science. 'Anecdotes' abound. I have already referred (Chapter 13) to the 'anecdotes' in Brian Masters's book on *Dreams about H.M. the Queen*. There seems to be more than we thought in the bright journalism about the monarchy as symbol (the late Kingsley Martin on *The Magic of Monarchy*)[3], the coronation as ritual. The myths are there to hand, the television revives them weekly and adds new ones. But we are weak in constitutional doctrine, and undoubtedly much of what we have is open to attack as 'false consciousness', the defence of an obsolescent society. But Marxist doctrine requires that symbolic structures should be arising in phase with changes in the relations of production; and it is not very easy to descry these. True, there are plenty of scattered examples out of which we can make anecdotes: the myths established by television serials; the rituals and symbols of the football followers and pop fans; the craze for designing symbols or ideograms for British Railways, British Steel and so on, and for big private firms such as I.C.I.; the popularity of exotic mini-religions; the fairly well understood techniques of advertising and public relations, involving such factors as brand-image and brand-loyalty.

These are relevant examples, but shallow ones in relation to life-and-death questions of political identity. One must think at

2. Revised ed., Collier, New York, 1961.   3. Nelson, 1937.

once of Ireland, and in particular of Ulster. There one has an extreme case in which the supposedly material factors, the logic of economics and geography, fail to work, and the local identities are so strong that those who claim to fight for the 'Catholics' refuse to accept the guidance of the Catholic Church, those who call themselves 'British Loyalists' feel no loyalty to the government of 'Britain'. There are two perceptions of the same places and events; each strengthens the other by offering conflict and conflicting image; each has as rich a store of myth, symbol, ritual and dogma as any recorded tribe. Could there be stronger identities ? Yet even these become complex on closer inspection: neither of the identities is monolithic, within each there are lesser groupings, not strong enough to bridge the gap, not so weak that one feels despair about an eternal antithesis of obsolete identities.

Social scientists are not ignorant or insensitive about these factors. But the best quantitative instrument, that of the attitude survey, has certain built-in disadvantages, and tends merely to confirm what we already know (or think we know), or at least not to discredit it. It has not the 'fine tuning' possible for the imaginative writer, and poets and playwrights have gone further than social scientists in understanding and explanation, and per- haps further in therapy also. It is not therefore surprising that the best technique yet developed for handling these complex patterns is that of the individual interview in depth, as developed by R. E. Lane in his study of American ideology 'at the grass roots'.[4] No one who had read his book and in particular its methodological appendices could have the face to complain that it is 'unscholarly'; and it is appropriate for Lane to develop in this field the techniques of psychoanalysis, in that the theory and language of identity and of identifications owe much to Freud,

4. *Political Ideology: Why the American Common Man Believes What He Does* (Free Press, New York, 1962). Two other books by R. E. Lane are also relevant: *Political Life; Why and How People Get Involved in Politics,* (Free Press, New York, 1959) and *Political Thinking and Consciousness* (Markham, Chicago, 1969). Political scientists should also note the work of Agger, Goldrich and Swainson on the tug of war between ideology and interests at local level: *The Rulers and the Ruled* (Wiley, New York, 1964), p. 426.

Jung and the next generation of their followers. But the same objections will be raised: that this requires long training, can reach few individual cases, is not validated by independent observation, and helps very little in prescribing therapy. Political science, unlike psychiatry, can offer no tranquillizers, and can only await natural remission of the disorder. But in politics the extinction of political identity is equivalent to the death of the patient.

A final word, harking back to the personal question of Scottish identity, which I invoked in the first chapter.

In the light of this discussion I understand better the strategy and tactics of political engineering which were involved in the creation over several hundred years of the political identities of France, Germany, Italy, the U.S.A. – and of Great Britain, *Magna Britannia*. Perhaps the Romans had that ambition, though they were forced by events to abandon it. Certainly it became an English ambition, as soon as English rulers grasped the geography of these islands. Clearly it was never a Scottish, Welsh or Irish ambition; politics does not work like that. But it was not an unworthy or disgraceful ambition, and it was on the whole worthily pursued, at least from the time of the Reformation, except in regard to Ireland. Certainly the treaty with Scotland in 1707, which for the first time created a United Kingdom, as distinct from a dual monarchy, was a bargain between sections of two interlocking oligarchies, and there was no nonsense about 'consulting the people'. But there were strong practical arguments from political interest, economic interest and geographic contiguity, and the advantages gained were not advantages only to the two establishments – though they did very well out of it.

These advantages were confirmed by brilliant economic and naval success in the eighteenth century. Scotland (which was almost ready to fight England in the 1690s over its abortive colony in central America) did quite as well as the English (speaking proportionately) out of imperial conquests and world trade. The cash bargain was honoured; but with it went a sophisticated attempt to create a new political identity, that of the British people.[5] Some, like Wilkes and his satirical paper the *North Briton*, were sarcastic about the Scots, but Edinburgh still embodies the eighteenth-century battle of identity: the North British Hotel at one end of Princes Street, the Caledonian Hotel at the other, objects of massive Victorian splendour, recalling a long past struggle between railway companies.

By 1815 'Britain' was secure strategically and economically, and England was predominant in industry and population, far more so than in the seventeenth century. It is an odd coincidence that at this point 'North Britain' vanished from the books (though the Post Office sustained it for a long time) and Caledonia came back to favour, blown by the winds of the Romantic Movement. All sorts of factors combined to revive Scottish identity (often in ridiculous forms) when it should have been ready to disappear: Macpherson's Ossian, the European fame of Burns, Scott and Byron, Mendelssohn and some odd Germanic ballets, George IV in a kilt, the *Edinburgh Review* ('English Bards and Scottish Reviewers'), the Edinburgh publishing houses. With this went the mythologizing of Scottish history, and the rather dismal rituals of Burns' Suppers and St Andrew's Night. The three Scottish professions, church, law and teaching, sustained their independence. Not without difficulty, the West of Scotland accepted a high proportion of Irish immigrants, and has perhaps at last begun to win the battle against the two Ulster identities. At least, the Glasgow buses boast the Orange and Green together; Celtic in Glasgow, Hibernian in Edinburgh are parts of Scottish identity, and even Rangers (who will still have no Catholic in the team) play in blue, not in orange.[6]

5. The *Glasgow Herald* of 24 March 1975 reproduces a sketch for a gigantic Mural by Sir James Thornhill, 'the history painter and sergeant painter to George I and II', on the subject of The Union:

Thornhill's scenario presents Minerva presiding over the Union, symbolized by two mature damsels coyly shaking hands, while to the left a figure is uniting the England and Scottish flags in the Union Jack. Down below, Neptune, for reasons not explained, is supporting a medallion of the reigning Queen Anne's husband, Prince George of Denmark.

6. And literature, laughing and weeping over the old quarrel, reaches large audiences: Hector MacMillan's play, *The Sash* (Molendinar Press, Glasgow,

Much could be written about Scottish symbols, ritual and mythology; and one might add that commonwealth and colonies were symbols of 'Britain', and that 'Britain' is rather an empty word now that they have have gone.

But ideology? A Scottish theory of nationality in general, of Scottish nationality in particular? Perhaps most of us would find something somewhere in the works of that old harlequin, skinchanger, Circumjack Cencrastus, Hugh MacDiarmid, C. M. Grieve.[7]

But for the excellence of the typical swift life no nation
Deserves to be remembered more than the sands of the sea.
I am only that Job in feathers, a heron myself,
Gaunt and unsubstantial – yet immune to the vicissitudes
Other birds accept as a matter of course; impervious to the effects
Of even the wildest weather, no mean consideration in a country
    like this;
And my appetite is not restricted to any particular fare.
Hence I am encountered in places far removed from one another
And widely different in an intimately topographical sense
– Spearing a rat at the mouth of a culvert at midnight
And bolting an eel on the seashore in the halflight of dawn –
Communal dweller yet lone hunter, lumbering yet swift and sustained
    flier,
The usual steely expression of my eyes does not flatter me;
Few birds perhaps have so successfully solved
The problem of existence as my grey lanky self
That in light or darkness, wet or shine, subsists
By a combination of alertness, patience, and passivity.
A kind of Caoilte mac Ronain[8] too; but it takes
    All my wits in Scotland to-day.

1974) and the film of Peter McDougall's *Just Another Saturday*, brilliantly produced by B.B.C. Scotland, 13 March 1975.

7. Lament for the Great Music; in Philip Larkin, ed., *The Oxford Book of Twentieth-Century English Verse* (Clarendon Press, 1973), pp. 274–5.

8. 'The grey spare swift runner, he who saved Fionn once by that wonderful feat of gathering couples of all the wild beasts and birds of Ireland (a ram and a crimson sheep from Inis, two water-birds from the Erne, two cormorants from the Cliath, two foxes from Slieve Gullion, and the rest).'

FURTHER READING

THE argument of this book led me to give great weight in the study of politics to the familiar triangle, myth-symbol-ritual, and I yoked to it ideology, giving that long-suffering word a limited contextual sense.

This may seem to be a poetic, even mystical, approach, proposed as an alternative to quantitative and behavioural analysis of politics. There is no such confrontation. Myths and symbols can be handled diagrammatically or by equations, in the manner of Levi-Strauss; and most linguistic problems lie open to quantitative treatment. This is a very rich source of quantifiable hypotheses, half neglected because of the process of academic specialization.

I am not sure that this gap can be filled by text-book writing. If I were to try, what follows would indicate the lines of my own 'further reading'.

1. Political scientists

If one sets ideology on one side, the list is short.

Edelman, Murray: *The Symbolic Uses of Politics* (Illinois University Press, 1964)

Edelman, Murray: *Politics as Symbolic Action: Mass Arousal and Quiescence* (Markham, Chicago, 1971)

Tudor, Henry: *Political Myth* (Pall Mall, 1972)

These refer to earlier sources in periodicals, and there are a few later articles.

2. The Classics

There is a connection between the notion of a myth (in this public sense) and the notion of a classic. Classics exist in all literate civilizations, I believe; certainly there are strong examples in Chinese, Indian, Arabic and Nordic systems of mythology.

Our own theorizing is based largely on Greek and Latin classics. The Jewish classics we have approached rather timidly, though Edmund Leach and Mary Douglas have tried it with good effect; and it is usually to nod respectfully towards other systems.

In the context of Greece and Rome, there are two quite distinct but essential themes:

(1) The extremely sophisticated use of myth, politically and ethically, by Pindar and the Athenian tragic poets; hence our Prometheus complex, as well as our Oedipus complex. The best modern work:

G. S. Kirk: *The Nature of Greek Myths* (Penguin, 1974)

G. S. Kirk: *Myth: Its Meaning and Functions in Ancient and Other Cultures* (Cambridge University Press, 1970)

E. R. Dodds: *The Greeks and the Irrational* (California University Press, 1951)

Hugh Lloyd-Jones: *The Justice of Zeus* (California University Press, 1971)

And notice Professor Lloyd-Jones's article on 'Wagner and the Greeks', *The Times Literary Supplement*, 9 January 1976, and a comment on it by Martin Cooper in the *Daily Telegraph*, 24 January 1976.

(2) The equally sophisticated attempt by Horace and Vergil (in totally different circumstances) to create a Roman imperial myth. At present, I know of no good general book on what these poets tried to do. They failed: within a century a series of shabby emperors had de-mythologized the Roman state, and had left the Mediterranean world open to a plurality of mythological systems. *In Tiberium defluxit Orontes*;[1] the Levantine river flooded out the Tiber.

3. Neo-Classicism and the Romantics

I have myself been much influenced by Mario Praz, *On Neo-classicism* (in Italian, 1940 and 1959; Thames & Hudson, 1969)

1. Juvenal, *Satires*, III, 62.

and the *Romantic Agony* (1933; 2nd edition 1951: Oxford University Press, 1970). But everyone must frame his own prejudices about imaginative work in the modern world.

My own preference is to point to the collision between Wagner and Nietzsche, and to try to understand it. Nietzsche was a fine classical scholar, who used Greek mythology as text for some dangerous generalizations about Apollonian and Dionysiac cultures. Wagner (as one view has it) tried and failed to exploit Nietzsche; he did 'exploit' (if that is the word to apply to genius) the almost universal European movement for the rediscovery of national languages and mythologies. No European country was untouched; for English speakers the paradigm case is that of Yeats and Ireland.

4. Parasites on Nietzsche

I risk grouping together Spengler, Othmar Spann, Houston Stewart Chamberlain, Arthur Rosenberg and perhaps Georges Sorel as 'precursors of Hitler'. But so far as I know, no one has yet tried to puzzle out what Hitler had heard and read by 1924 and how he transformed it into a rhetoric of power and violence.

5. The Scholars

(1) *The classics, awakened.* In the very rich years before 1914 there was a movement to broaden classical scholarship beyond philosophy, history, and textual criticism to include the study of disreputable elements in the tradition – such as myth, ritual and symbol. There was Nietzsche's friend Erwin Rohde in Germany on the myth of Psyche; Franz Cumont in France on the impact of Eastern religions in Rome; Martin Nilsson in Sweden; in England principally Jane Harrison and Francis Cornford (though one should mention also A. B. Cook on *Zeus*, H. M. Chadwick on *The Heroic Age*). This filtered through into literature, sometimes in odd ways – it acquired sexy rather than political overtones, as in the early novels of Naomi Mitchison

(and it is a pleasure to read what she writes in that field fifty years later).[2]

(2) *The systematizers* who got busy before the data were in; and indeed their systems have not so far been of a kind testable by putting questions to the data. Freud was the worst sinner; Cassirer could claim the licence granted to philosophers. Jung is puzzling; he casts his net very wide indeed, and has permanently enriched the subject – but he seems hostile to the question 'what proves what?' A vast amount has been written about Lévi-Strauss and his method – which appears to imply that about myth one cannot write except mythologically. And so with Roland Barthes, and, in a different style, Mircea Eliade. But these names and their influence are a warning that myth/symbol/ritual must be taken very seriously in any study of modern social and political thought.

(3) *The literary critics* and the analysis of these factors in imaginative writings. I have read with pleasure Kenneth Burke, Elizabeth Sewell, Northrop Frye, Philip Wheelwright; I. A. Richards on Rhetoric and William Empson on ambiguity are closely related. There must be many more.

(4) *The social anthropologists* who suit my argument best, in that they seek to exemplify the relations between symbol, myth, ritual and ideology in specific social contexts are, in particular: the late Max Gluckman, Edmund Leach, Victor Turner, Mary Douglas.

But one must, before theorizing, cultivate 'an ear'. The books help but do not offer a doctrine. One must listen to the rhythms and metaphors of political discourse.

2. Review of Carmen Blacker, *The Catalpa Bow* (Allen & Unwin, 1976): *Glasgow Herald*, 10 June 1976.

INDEX